Rethinking Online Anti-Gender Hate Speech

Providing an innovative approach to understanding and addressing anti-gender hate speech, this book focuses on its effects on everyday life, how it is handled within legal frameworks and how it challenges democratic principles.

Unlike previous research, which is often limited to currently regulated forms of hate speech, this book is focused on gender-based hate speech, demonstrating its broader social and ideological impacts. By contextualising freedom of expression within democratic values, it offers a new framework for addressing anti-gender hate speech as a threat to both individual dignity and societal diversity. Through this lens, the authors highlight how anti-gender hate speech represents not only a breach of individual rights but also a structural challenge to democracy, requiring responses that reflect these dual dimensions. The book provides a unique contribution to both legal scholarship and democratic theory by rethinking the balance between gender equality and freedom of expression as cooperative as well as inherently contextual and inclusive.

Rethinking Online Anti-Gender Hate Speech will be of great interest to students and scholars in the field of criminology, law, media and communication, sociology, and women's and gender studies.

Moa Bladini is Associate Professor and Senior Lecturer at the Department of Law at the University of Gothenburg, Sweden. Her research focuses on criminal law and criminal procedure law, with a particular emphasis on sexual and gender-based violence, both online and offline. Recurring themes in her work include power, objectivity, and legitimisation strategies in judicial activity. She has been part of several comparative projects analysing Nordic and European legislation, and she has an extensive experience of interdisciplinary research projects.

Eva-Maria Svensson is Professor Emerita at the Department of Law at the University of Gothenburg, Sweden. Her research is mainly concentrated on legal philosophy and theory, particularly in the field of feminist/gender legal studies, gender equality law and policy and freedom of speech. Professor Svensson also does research in the fields of ageing and capability, gender equality in the Arctic as well as studies of academic knowledge in law. She participates in several research networks, in jurisprudence, feminist/gender studies, socio-legal studies, critical legal studies, free speech issues, such as the international network on gender equality.

Directions and Developments in Criminal Justice and Law

https://www.routledge.com/Directions-and-Developments-in-Criminal-Justice-and-Law/book-series/DDCJL

The ways in which crime is constructed in society is of time-honored interest to criminologists across the globe. The ever-changing landscape of what is criminal and what is not affects scholars and policymakers in their approach to the body of law defining prohibited conduct, how that law evolves, and the modes by which it is administered. Rule of law cannot exist without a transparent legal system, strong enforcement structures, and an independent judiciary to protect against the arbitrary use of power. Critical consideration of the mechanisms through which societies attempt to make the rule of law a reality is essential to understanding and developing effectual criminal justice systems. The *Directions and Developments in Criminal Justice and Law* series offers the best research on criminal justice and law around the world, offering original insights on a broadly defined range of socio-legal topics in law, criminal procedure, courts, justice, legislation, and jurisprudence. With an eye toward using innovative and advanced methodologies, series monographs offer solid social science scholarship illuminating issues and trends in law, crime, and justice. Books in this series will appeal to criminologists, sociologists, and other social scientists, as well as policymakers, legal researchers, and practitioners.

18. **Wrongful Convictions and the Criminalization of Innocence**
    International Perspectives on Contributing Factors, Models of Exoneration and Case Studies
    Edited by Kathryn M. Campbell, Barak Ariel, Anat Horovitz and Irwin Colter

19. **Transitional Justice and the Criminal Responsibility of Judges**
    Edited by Claudia Cárdenas, Jaime Cousos, Florian Jeßberger and Milan Kuhli

20. **Rethinking Online Anti-Gender Hate Speech**
    Legislation and Public Policy Making
    Moa Bladini and Eva-Maria Svensson

Rethinking Online Anti-Gender Hate Speech

Legislation and Public Policy Making

Moa Bladini and Eva-Maria Svensson

Routledge
Taylor & Francis Group
LONDON AND NEW YORK

First published 2025
by Routledge
4 Park Square, Milton Park, Abingdon, Oxon OX14 4RN

and by Routledge
605 Third Avenue, New York, NY 10158

Routledge is an imprint of the Taylor & Francis Group, an informa business

British Library Cataloguing-in-Publication Data
A catalogue record for this book is available from the British Library

Library Cataloguing-in-Publication Data
Names: Bladini, Moa, 1979– author | Svensson, Eva-Maria author
Title: Rethinking online anti-gender hate speech : legislation and public policy making / Moa Bladini, Eva-Maria Svensson.
Description: Abingdon, Oxon [UK] ; New York, NY : Routledge, 2025. |
Series: Directions & developments in criminal justice & law |
Includes bibliographical references and index.
Identifiers: LCCN 2024061078 (print) | LCCN 2024061079 (ebook) |
ISBN 9781032467450 hardback | ISBN 9781032467474 paperback |
ISBN 9781003383062 ebook
Subjects: LCSH: Online hate speech–Law and legislation | Hate crimes–Law and legislation | Hate speech–Law and legislation | Freedom of expression |
Sex discrimination–Law and legislation
Classification: LCC KZ7177.H38 B53 2025 (print) |
LCC KZ7177.H38 (ebook) | DDC 342.08/53–dc23/eng/20250202
LC record available at https://lccn.loc.gov/2024061078
LC ebook record available at https://lccn.loc.gov/2024061079

ISBN: 9781032467450 (hbk)
ISBN: 9781032467474 (pbk)
ISBN: 9781003383062 (ebk)

DOI: 10.4324/9781003383062

Typeset in Sabon
by Newgen Publishing UK

An electronic version of this book is freely available, thanks to the support of libraries working with Knowledge Unlatched (KU). KU is a collaborative initiative designed to make high quality books Open Access for the public good. The Open Access ISBN for this book is 9781003383062. More information about the initiative and links to the Open Access version can be found at www.knowledgeunlatched.org

Contents

Preface

This book is an offspring and an update of the research produced within the project 'Hate Speech, Gender, Social Networks and Political Parties' (GENHA) co-funded by the European Union during the years 2020–2022. The project was a collaboration among researchers from five European countries and universities: Germany and Universität Erfurt, Hungary and the Central European University, Italy and Alma Mater Studiorum Universita de Bologna, Spain and the Universitat Autònoma de Barcelona, and Sweden and the University of Gothenburg. Four reports were produced and published, while the wider intentions to publish scholarly texts were delayed by the very specific circumstances coming with the pandemic hindering the research team to even meet. Almost three years later, parts of the research group have concluded a monograph addressing the regulation on anti-gender hate speech.

Through several policies and laws, bodies like the UN, Council of Europe and EU express their concern about anti-gender hate speech, both offline and online, and challenge the states to act against it. On the national level the degree of willingness seems to be less impressive. Even countries like Sweden, a former role model for gender equality, is hesitant. Recent obliging initiatives taken by EU will hopefully change this reluctance. This book shows a fragmented regulation.

The authors would like to thank two of the participants from the GENHA project for their contributions with information about the regulation in Spain and Italy, respectively, Professor Noelia Igareda González and Professor Raffaella Sette. We would also like to thank Professor Jacob Öberg who has read and commented on parts of the text.

We would also like to thank the University of Gothenburg for providing writing retreat through travel scholarship in 2024.

Abbreviations

BrB	*Brottsbalk* (Swedish Criminal Code)
CEDAW	Convention on the Elimination of All Forms of Discrimination against Women
CSW	UN Commission on the Status of Women
DSA	Digital Services Act
ECHR	European Convention for the Protection of Human Rights and Fundamental Freedoms
EEA	European Economic Area
EIGE	European Institute for Gender Equality
EU	European Union
GENHA	Hate Speech, Gender, Social Networks and Political Parties
GREVIO	The Group of Experts on Action against Violence against Women and Domestic Violence
ICCPR	International Covenant on Civil and Political Rights
ICERD	International Convention on the Elimination of All Forms of Racial Discrimination
ICESCR	International Covenant on Economic, Social and Cultural Rights
ICT	information and communications technology
RF	*Regeringsformen* (The Instrument of Government)
TEU	Treaty on European Union
TF	*Tryckfrihetsförordningen* (The Freedom of the Press Act)
TFEU	Treaty on the Functioning of the European Union
UDHR	Universal Declaration of Human Rights
UK	United Kingdom
UN	United Nations
UNESCO	United Nations Educational, Scientific and Cultural Organization
USA	United States of America
YGL	*Yttrandefrihetsgrundlagen* (The Fundamental Act on Freedom of Expression)

1 Introduction

Anti-gender hate speech

1.1 Introducing the theme

Trigger warning

> 'For me, gender equality is to finger a sexist feminist whore in the vagina, with a big knife. The best thing you can do for gender equality in Sweden is to go out with a baseball bat and beat a sexist feminist scum to death.'
>
> (Quote from a judgment in the Swedish Court of Appeal[1])

This is an authentic quote that illustrates the severe and aggressive hate present online in Sweden, and elsewhere, today. This quoted comment was a response to a chronicle on gender equality written by a young female journalist. The chronicle was published online, accompanied by a comment section where the remark was posted. The statement in the comment was prosecuted under Swedish criminal law. The charge was brought as molestation (*ofredande*), as no other offence was applicable, despite its serious and violent nature. While the District Court found the perpetrator guilty, the Court of Appeal acquitted him as they argued that the comment did not fall under the definition of molestation nor any other criminal offence but suggested that the legislator should review the relevant criminal law.

It is worth noting that the case is almost ten years old, and a legislative process has taken place since then, aiming to amend the law to encompass statements like the one quoted, and various other forms of digital harassments, such as non-consensual pornography. Despite the revision of the criminal law, there are still challenges and deficiencies in legal protection, particularly in how the law currently addresses anti-gender hate speech (Nordref 2023).

At the time, the Court of Appeal argued that the comment was an isolated event, not part of a recurring pattern generally required to constitute molestation. The court further noted that the comment followed

DOI: 10.4324/9781003383062-1

a chronicle intended to spark debate, implying that offensive responses might be anticipated. This reasoning suggests the court considered it reasonable for the journalist to tolerate more hate than others.

In a more recent case, where a public debater received a so-called 'dick pic' and the perpetrator argued that the victim's status as a public figure should mitigate the offence, the court took the opposite view. The District Court deemed this an aggravating circumstance, leading to a harsher sentence.[2] This decision may reflect a shift in judicial attitudes toward online abuse targeting individuals engaged in public debate, aligning with evolving policy frameworks addressing such issues.

This shift is particularly noteworthy as it may relate to differing interpretations of freedom of expression – specifically, its negative aspect (non-censorship) and positive aspect (guaranteeing a diversity of voices) as dealt with in criminal law. The first case appears to focus solely on the individual and the principle of non-censorship, whereas the second case can be seen as emphasizing the protection and preservation of a diversity of voices, with particular attention to those in professional roles.[3]

Online anti-gender hate speech is a global phenomenon impacting both individual everyday life, societies and democratic processes. Anti-gender hate speech presents urgent issues across several dimensions and has in recent years received intensified attention; UN has even called it a 'shadow pandemic' (UN Women 2020). It gives rise to serious problems in at least three aspects: practical everyday life, legal and democratic. At the same time, the example above from a Swedish context illustrates two tendencies going in different directions: firstly, a hesitancy to recognise anti-gender hate speech as a serious issue and a criminal offence, and secondly, a gradual shift in the perception of the importance of protecting democratic discourse over time. In this book, we discuss how these issues can be understood and approached from a legal perspective.

The phenomenon concerns freedom of expression[4] and gender equality as two cornerstones of democratic society. These values might be seen as contradictory or as mutually strengthening. This book argues that, to uphold and strengthen democracy, we must re-evaluate the relationship between freedom of expression and gender equality – not as opposing forces but as compatible and collaborative principles. This includes rethinking freedom of expression as not merely a prohibition against censorship but as a democratic responsibility to foster an inclusive and diverse public discourse where freedom of expression and gender equality can coexist. A democratic state has an obligation to foster a pluralistic and inclusive environment where marginalised perspectives are heard, valued, and protected, ensuring all voices contribute to a robust and equitable public dialogue.

Online anti-gender hate speech benefits from and takes place in a context of advanced technology. In today's digital age, where much of our personal and public lives are lived online, democracy faces both unprecedented opportunities and serious challenges. The internet has enabled movements like #MeToo, amplifying voices and mobilising support for gender equality on a global scale. Yet, the same digital spaces have become fertile ground for hate and threats, particularly anti-gender hate speech that targets those advocating for gender rights, by some called the anti-gender movement (EIGE 2022; Kuhar & Paternotte 2017). According to the UN Working Group on Discrimination against Women and Girls there has in recent years been a clear backlash for women's rights and the use of the term gender, with attacks claiming a 'gender ideology' is wrongly imposed (United Nations Human Rights Special Procedures 2020).

Online anti-gender hate speech undermines individuals' ability to freely express themselves online and poses a significant threat to the diversity of public discourse by silencing voices (see, e.g., European Institute for Gender Equality 2020). Contrary to the common perception that it creates complex legal tensions between freedom of expression and gender equality, we argue that this framing is misleading. Being silenced entails avoiding communication due to threats, verbal or physical attacks, or subtler forms of harassment.[5]

Regulatory measures at international, regional, and national levels can either facilitate or restrict the prevalence of anti-gender hate speech. Historically, online abuse has been trivialised as 'merely virtual' and therefore inconsequential. Similarly, less overt forms of violence against women have often been dismissed or not taken seriously. These attitudes may explain why anti-gender hate speech only recently gained recognition as a regulatory priority.

Today, however, anti-gender hate speech is increasingly addressed at multiple levels and is often classified as a form of violence against women (European Commission, COM(2022) 105 final 2022/0066 (COD)). It is also increasingly recognised as a barrier to freedom of expression, particularly when the obligation to promote a diversity of voice is considered.

This book explores the regulation of online anti-gender hate speech, encompassing both legal and policy frameworks. The phenomenon is examined through an international lens, with a focus on relevant international regulations, with a particular focus on the EU and some of its member states. Our analysis is informed by findings from the EU-funded GENHA project, which investigated five European countries: Germany, Hungary, Italy, Spain, and Sweden. While Italy, Spain, and Sweden are most prominently referenced, Sweden serves as the central example.

There are two key reasons for this emphasis on Sweden. First, Sweden possesses an extensive legal framework on freedom of expression (Kenyon, Svensson & Edström 2017). Second, it consistently ranks highly in global gender equality indexes (Hellum et al. 2024). These principles – freedom of expression and gender equality – are deeply embedded in Sweden's democratic tradition. Freedom of expression, which includes both non-censorship and the promotion of a diversity of voices, is historically regarded as a 'common good'. The concept of the common good, as a justification for the use of criminal law, will be explored in greater depth in Chapter 2. Meanwhile, gender equality is recognised as requiring active measures to be fully realised.

Sweden's unique position is further underscored by its declaration as the first nation with a feminist government (Skr. 2016/17: 10). This commitment heightens the expectations for the country to ensure that women's voices are protected from being silenced (Bladini 2020).

The current Spanish government also proclaims itself feminist, and it is the third time Spain has a Ministry of Equality. In 2014, President Rodríguez Zapatero formed the first government with gender parity, appointing an equal number of women and men as ministers. This government was explicitly feminist and proudly declared its commitment to advancing gender equality, marked by the establishment of the Ministry of Equality.

The current situation in Italy presents a somewhat different scenario; even though, Georgia Meloni, the prime minister of Italy and the leader of 'Fratelli d'Italia' ('Brothers of Italy'), introduces herself as 'a woman, a mother, a Christian' she is not a feminist (Serughetti 2024). Together with the party she reinforces the traditional family and characterised by the strategical use of the defence of women's rights to support anti-immigration and conservative issues (De Giorgi, Cavalieri & Feo 2023).

Anti-gender hate speech manifests both online and offline. However, the online dimension presents unique challenges, particularly due to the rapid dissemination of speech and the complexities of regulation. Investigating online crimes often proves difficult, particularly in identifying the offender. Determining the ownership of specific accounts is a significant hurdle, as platform providers are frequently located in other jurisdictions, complicating access to critical information (Bladini & NIKK 2017).

Given the global nature of this phenomenon, effective regulation necessitates international cooperation, which is not always feasible. Even within a single jurisdiction, such as Sweden, the legal framework for freedom of expression varies depending on the medium in which the speech occurs (Carlsson 2024). This issue will be elaborated further in Chapter 3.

Our primary focus is on *online* anti-gender hate speech, and unless otherwise stated, this will be the subject of the following discussion.

Why is this book necessary? We argue that addressing the fragmented nature of regulation, its evolution over time, and its variation across jurisdictions is essential for developing a more cohesive and reflective approach to the phenomenon. Re thinking the legal framework surrounding anti-gender hate speech has the potential to foster more respectful communication, thereby strengthening democracy and ensuring a diversity of voices.

In this chapter, we provide a *background* by briefly describing the problem and *explaining* its urgency. We introduce the concept of anti-gender hate speech and examine the challenges it poses in everyday life, within legal contexts, and from a democratic perspective. Furthermore, we discuss relevant previous research and outlines this book's contributions to the field. Finally, we present the *structure* of the book.

1.2 Anti-gender hate speech

Anti-gender hate speech gives rise to serious challenges across at least three dimensions. The first is practical, affecting individuals everyday lives. It shapes whether and how people engage online, influencing their ability express themselves and avoid being subjected to offensive actions or expressions. The second is legal, often framed as a clash between the principles of gender equality and freedom of expression. The third is democratic, highlighting how restrictions on women's participation in public discourse silence voices, exclude certain groups from debates, and erode the diversity of public dialogue. These challenges urgently demand thorough exploration, and a critical assessment of the extent to which they can be mitigated through legal and political measures.

While the concept of hate speech has been acknowledged in a legal context for some time, *anti-gender hate speech* has yet to be formally established as a distinct legal concept. Nonetheless, recognition of the phenomenon has been increasingly evident in various political and legal frameworks. The lack of a unified definition of hate speech complicates matters further (Lagiewska 2024). Disagreements persist over severity, the types of actions it encompasses, and the characteristics protected under its scope. Historically, gender and sex were excluded from these definitions, and even today, some jurisdictions either do not include these categories or only recognise them to a limited extent.

As a result, the protection offered to individuals and groups varies widely. The concept of hate speech cannot, therefore, be applied without careful examination of its definition and implications. In this book, we take the starting point in the definition of hate speech provided by the European Commission against Racism and Intolerance (ECRI) in its General Policy Recommendation no. 15, as our point of departure:

> Considering that hate speech is to be understood for the purpose of the present General Policy Recommendation as the advocacy, promotion or incitement, in any form, of the denigration, hatred or vilification of a person or group of persons, as well as any harassment, insult, negative stereotyping, stigmatization or threat in respect of such a person or group of persons and the justification of all the preceding types of expression, on the ground of 'race', colour, descent, national or ethnic origin, age, disability, language, religion or belief, sex, gender, gender identity, sexual orientation and other personal characteristics or status.

It should be noted that other definitions will also be explored and discussed later in the text; see Chapter 2 for a more detailed analysis.

The discussions in the book will address the legal and regulatory challenges associated with the three core dimensions – everyday life, law and democracy – by examining the interplay between gender equality, freedom of expression, and criminal law. Gender equality and freedom of expression are foundational principles of democracy, enshrined in constitutional provisions, while criminal law serves as a crucial tool in combating hate speech.

1.2.1 Everyday life challenges

Most people in the Western world engage with the internet daily. While digital communication offers numerous benefits, it also presents significant drawbacks. The internet connects individuals across the globe, but unlike physical interactions, messages online spread rapidly to vast and often undefined audiences. This blurring of the boundary between public and private life opens new pathways for harassment and abuse.

Four defining characteristics of online communication amplify the effects of online hate. First, the physical and temporal distance between sender and recipient diminishes empathy and accountability, encouraging impulsive and offensive remarks with minimal perceived consequences (Suler 2004). Second, anonymity facilitates harmful speech without accountability. While it can protect vulnerable individuals, it also enables abuse by allowing perpetrators to evade responsibility (Dunkels 2016). Third, constant connectivity via smartphones exposes individuals to potential abuse at any time, even in private spaces, and fosters impulsive hostility (Brovall & Christiansen 2013). Finally, the persistent nature of online hate leaves a lasting impact; once shared, harmful content can be saved and redistributed, perpetuating a 'lifelong violation' for victims (Sunde 2006; CJEU 2014).

Online communication, whether intentional or spontaneous, may target specific recipients or reach broad, undefined audiences. Messages can originate from individuals or groups, either organised or reactive (De Smedt et al. 2018). Anti-gender hate speech highlights these challenges, exposing gaps in legal protections that fail to address the unique impact of digital communication for targeted groups.

Even though there is a growing body of feminist scholarship on online misogyny, hate speech against women online has been limitedly studied, particularly among legal scholars (Antigona Research Group 2020). While hate speech is an established research topic within law, the majority of work focuses on categories such as race and ethnicity and rarely addresses gender as a basis for hate (Antigona Research Group 2020). In contrast, there is a growing body of interdisciplinary research examining online misogyny as part of everyday life, particularly its impact on women's voices and participation in digital spaces. Many of these scholarly works span multiple disciplines and address various challenges. We structure the following sections according to the challenges they concern.

Expressions that some individuals viewed as a fundamental aspect of their freedom of expression may be experienced by others as offensive and silencing. Women worldwide are regularly subjected to anti-gender hate speech on social media platforms as part of everyday life (UNESCO & Broadband Commission 2013; UN Women 2020; Bladini 2020; Vickery & Everbach 2018). The impact of online sexual violence on everyday life has been studied by Citron (2009) and Bladini (2020); see also Powell, Flynn and Suguira (2021).

A philosophical analysis of online anti-gender hate speech, examining its impact on women as a group and how it constrains their ability to engage in digital spaces, has been offered by Richardson-Self (2018, 2021). Her work raises questions on the nature, targets, and countermeasures of such speech, suggesting that it not only harms individuals but also reinforces broader ideological constraints on gender equality. This perspective is crucial to our analysis.

While Richardson-Self touches on legal responses, her analysis is primarily philosophical and lacks a European or Nordic legal perspective, which this book aims to provide. Additionally, we expand on her framework by situating anti-gender hate speech within a legal context, examining its alignment with internationally recognised principles of freedom of expression, gender equality, and democratic discourse.

Research shows that exposure to anti-gender hate speech has a silencing effect (Als Research 2015; Tolstrup Holm 2015; Edström 2016; Amnesty International 2018; Bladini & NIKK 2017, 2020; BOM 2021). The impact of online sexual violence on everyday life has been studied by Citron (2009) and Bladini (2020). The concept of everyday life in relation to offline sexual violence, particularly rape, has been explored by Bladini and Svedberg Andersson (2020). Sexual violence manifests in various forms and degrees of severity, which are interconnected.

McGlynn, Rackley and Houghton (2017) introduce the concept of a continuum of violence in online spaces, describing image-based abuse as part of a broader spectrum of gendered violence. While not specifically addressing anti-gender hate speech, their continuum framework is instrumental in understanding the pervasive nature of online harassment, which is reflected in our analysis of anti-gender hate speech as a form of systemic, gendered violence. Other researchers highlight that anti-gender hate speech functions as a continuum of violence, impacting women's freedom and self-expression, particularly in online environments (e.g. McGlynn, Rackley & Houghton 2017; Morini 2024). This continuum not only applies but also parallels research on gender-based violence in offline contexts.

The continuum of violence is also the focus of research on gender-based violence offline (e.g. Lundgren et al. 2002; Fileborn & Vera-Grey 2017). Nielsen (2004) explores street harassment, framing it as 'offensive public speech' embedded within broader systems of social inequality. Nielsen argues that law can serve to normalise harassment, effectively providing a 'license to harass'. This early analysis connects offensive speech to power structures – a foundational insight we expand upon by situating anti-gender hate speech within democratic theory and examining how it obstructs gender equality.

1.2.2 Legal challenges

Societal problems are addressed through diverse legal means and across various legal fields. Anti-gender hate speech engages at least three legal fields, criminal law, freedom of expression and gender equality.

Hate speech is a matter of criminal law, as it may constitute a form of hate crime. Criminal regulation is essentially imposed control and state violence and should be used restrictively. Only when the principles of criminalisation can justify such regulation may it be used. We will elaborate on the principles of harm, common good and public wrong, see Chapter 2. The concept of hate crime encompasses various acts targeting individuals or groups based on prejudice against characteristics such as ethnicity, religion, sexual orientation, or similar grounds. Hate speech can thus be viewed as a specific type of hate crime.

While criminal law has historically been a national matter, it has increasingly become subject to international and regional demands. Examples include the Convention on the Elimination of All Forms of Discrimination against Women (CEDAW), the Istanbul Convention and the newly adopted EU Directive on Violence against Women (Directive (EU) 2024/1385). These demands on national regulation can be direct or indirect and often intersect with different policy fields, contributing to a fragmented legal landscape.

There is also a debate on when and how criminal law should be used as a preventive measure. At the EU level, this debate has centred on which crimes qualify as *core crimes* under EU jurisdiction (Öberg 2024). In the Nordic context, there is a growing tendency to rely on criminal law as a solution to societal problems (Anderberg, Martinsson & Svensson 2022).[6] However, the willingness to use criminal law appears to vary depending on the nature of the issue, with indications of gender bias. Efforts to include gender as a ground för hate crimes and hate speech regulation have faced resistance in Sweden (SOU 2023: 80; Granström 2016). Similarly, measures to address men's violence against women, such as the adoption of consent-based rape legislation, have met with reluctance (Prop. 2017/18: 177; Leijonhufvud 2015).

Anti-gender hate speech engages both freedom of expression and gender equality, as it constitutes a form of speech and is simultaneously characterised as gender stereotypical, a manifestation of violence against women, and an obstacle to achieving gender equality. Both freedom of expression and gender equality are foundational elements of democracy. Although established in different times, both have long been recognised as legal principles in various international and national conventions and constitutions. However, their interpretations vary across contexts.

Freedom of expression can be understood narrowly as non-censorship, emphasising the individual's right to express themselves without restriction. Alternatively, it can be interpreted more broadly, requiring active state measures to safeguard a diversity of voices. Similarly, gender equality can be viewed as limited to formal non-discrimination or as necessitating active measures to achieve substantive equality. A transformative interpretation goes even further, requiring states to actively eliminate gender inequality.

How anti-gender hate speech is addressed within regulations varies over time and between jurisdictions. Increasingly, it has been argued to be severe enough to warrant inclusion in hate speech regulation, alongside expressions targeting ethnicity or sexual orientation. However, such arguments often encounter resistance rooted in a narrow understanding of freedom of expression, which frames any regulation as a limitation of this freedom. This reluctance to regulate anti-gender hate speech is partly due to how the protection for freedom of expression is interpreted and applied (Kenyon, Svensson & Edström 2017; Edström 2016; Bladini 2020).

A common perception is that regulating anti-gender hate speech creates a conflict between an extensive freedom of expression and legal measures against such speech, making it a restriction of freedom of expression (see, e.g., Bakken 2000). Such a narrow interpretation of freedom of expression, as primarily or solely non-censorship, often dominates. Consequently, freedom of expression is frequently given precedence over gender equality when the two principles are balanced (Svensson & Edström 2014).

In this book, we challenge this understanding. Rather than advocating for a different balance, we suggest that freedom of expression and gender equality are compatible when understood in alignment with their justifications as foundational principles of democracy.

Current literature on anti-gender hate speech is limited, particularly in the legal sphere. Barker and Jurasz (2019) examine the regulation of online misogyny within the UK context, focusing on social media abuse, legal responses, and the categorisation of gender abuse as hate crime. Our book complements this by examining the Swedish and EU legal frameworks, adding a broader European perspective and situating anti-gender hate speech within a democratic context. Zempi and Smith (2022) explore misogyny both online and offline with an intersectional lens and discuss proposed reforms on hate crime, also in a UK context. They do not, however, consider gender equality or freedom of expression as democratic prerequisites, principles central to our approach. Our book thus reinterprets the fragmented political discourse on anti-gender hate speech and integrates it into a democratic framework (Svensson & Bladini 2021).

Legal scholars have engaged in other forms of expressions that constitute violence against women, such as pornography (MacKinnon 1996; Kraus 1993; Svensson 1995), and sex-discriminatory advertisement (Svensson & Edström 2014; Sundström & Käll 2019). Angelari (1993) suggested early, even before the UN had done so, that hate crime statutes could be used as a tool to combat violence against women. Defining hateful expressions as violence may also challenge their categorisation as *speech*. Instead, MacKinnon (1996) argues they should be seen as acts, which cannot wrongfully be protected as speech by constitutional provisions. Another aspect raised by Flahvin (1995) informs our analysis. Flahvin argues that hate speech impacts not only individuals but also self-governance processes, supporting our view that anti-gender hate speech extends beyond individual harm.

Much of legal literature on hate speech and hate crime, not the least in a Swedish context, is limited to the forms of hate speech that currently are subject to legal regulation (race, ethnicity, sexuality, etc.; Wigerfelt, Wigerfelt & Dahlstrand 2015; Granström, Mellgren & Tiby 2019; Hagerlid & Granström 2023). Brax (2016) argues in favour of hate speech regulations, by exploring the point that hate speech does harm by undermining the speech of targeted groups and by considering the distribution of costs and benefits for allowing hate speech, which is unlikely to be fair or equal. The harm caused by hate speech primarily befalls people that are already among the worst off in our society. There are a few examples that focus on gender and hate crime (Granström 2016; Bladini & NIKK 2017; SOU 2023: 80). Gerstenfeld (2017) and Pezzella and Fetzer (2021), two US-focused textbooks provide a broad analysis of hate crime and its impact, although they do not specifically address anti-gender hate speech. Gerstenfeld's work applies a multidisciplinary perspective, examining the community impact of hate crimes, while Pezzella and Fetzer focus on the underreporting of hate crime. Brown and Sinclair (2020) analyse hate speech laws within UK and US contexts, drawing on legal, political, and ethical frameworks. All these studies highlight the limitations of current frameworks, underscoring the need for our book's unique focus on anti-gender hate speech as both a gendered and systemic issue.

A legal study on online communication under the constitutional protection of freedom of expression is provided by Carlsson (2024). It is a comparative study covering Sweden, Germany, and USA. Although anti-gender hate speech is not specifically addressed, the study is highly relevant to our work because of its thorough examination of freedom of expression, its justifications, and its comprehensive analysis of regulations addressing online communication.

1.2.3 Democratic challenges

Silencing of women's voices due to anti-gender hate speech is a democratic problem and a violation of women's rights. It constitutes an infringement on women's living space and a breach against their human rights. When certain voices are silenced, their opportunities to participate in public debates are undermined, reducing the diversity of discourse. Freedom of expression, as fundamental pillar of democracy, is not only a negative right protecting individual freedoms but also a positive right requiring state action to ensure a diversity of voices.

The principle extends beyond guaranteeing individual rights to include the broader context – a democratic society in which freedom of expression occurs. Democracy in a broader sense requires not only freedom of expression as an individual right but also as an environment that actively promotes participation and ensures a diversity of voices. We connect to the international literature emphasising the democratic rationale of free speech (Kenyon, Svensson & Edström 2017). Such democracy presupposes a system that recognise speech acts as inherently contextual (Kenyon, Svensson & Edström 2017).

In this book, we challenge the view of freedom of expression as solely an individual right that the state must not restrict. Instead, we present an alternative balance between the two legitimate democratic interests and the primacy of the individual perspective. Our research, focusing on democratic challenges posed by anti-gender hate speech, aligns with broader challenges faced by democratic societies when fundamental principles like freedom of expression and gender equality clash (Svensson & Edström 2014).

Scholars such as Kenyon, Svensson and Edström (2017) argue that democratic freedom of expression must be understood contextually, requiring a diversity of voices to function. Building on this, we frame anti-gender hate speech as an obstacle to democracy itself. This perspective contrasts with previous studies, which often treat hate speech as a violation of individual rights without addressing its broader societal implications. By situating anti-gender hate speech within a democratic framework, we highlight its threat to inclusive, representative discourse.

Viewing anti-gender hate speech as a democratic problem is increasingly important given the rise of anti-gender ideologies. Richardson-Self (2018) states that hate speech is one of the most significant conceptual categories in anti-oppression politics today. According to her, considerable energy and political will are devoted to identifying, characterising, contesting, and (at times) penalising hate speech.

However, despite the growing recognition of gender identity as a socially salient trait, antipatriarchal politics has largely been absent within this body of scholarship. Richardson-Self suggests that situating patriarchy-enforcing speech within the category of hate speech is an important politico-philosophical project.

Hate and harassment online, directed at various professionals and leading to silenced voices is a democratic problem. Female journalists are particularly exposed (Posetti, Harrison & Waisbord 2020; Edström 2016), as are politicians (Kaati, Akrami & Pelzer 2018; Bayer & Bard 2020; IPU PACE 2018) and female opinion leaders (Eriksson Almgren, Ekblad & Sjörén 2017). Empirical evidence shows that these attacks are not solely carried out by individuals targeting specific women, but often involve organised and political groups. These groups target individual women, collectives of women, and gender equality as a societal goal and legal principle. Such groups commonly categorised under the concept of anti-gender movement (Kuhar & Paternotte 2017; Graff & Korolczuk 2022).

There is a growing body of literature on anti-gender and anti-feminist ideologies. While this research does not specifically address hate speech, it focuses on these movements' connections to nationalistic and/or racist ideologies (see, e.g., Giritli Nygren, Martinsson & Mulinari 2018; Graff & Korolczuk 2022; Kuhar & Paternotte 2017; Lilja & Johansson 2018; Mulinari & Nergaard 2017; Eriksson 2013; Kováts & Pető 2017; Norocel 2018; see also Antigona Research Group 2020).

Democracy in a broader sense, as indicated here and elaborated upon in Chapter 2, requires active engagement from states and other governing bodies at international, regional and national levels. Guaranteeing individual formal rights is not sufficient; democracy, understood as participatory and guaranteeing a diversity of voices, must be actively promoted through policies and regulations that balance competing interests.

Anti-gender hate speech, as a significant threat to democracy, has begun to gain attention at regional and international political levels (further elaborated in Chapter 3). However, many countries still lack adequate regulations or sufficient knowledge to effectively address anti-gender hate speech on social media platforms (Citron 2009; Bladini & NIKK 2017).

1.3 Overview and structure of the book

This book provides an innovative approach to understanding and addressing anti-gender hate speech, focusing on its effects on everyday life, how it is handled within legal frameworks, and how it challenges democratic principles. Unlike previous research, which often limits itself to currently regulated forms of hate speech, our analysis includes gender-based hate speech, demonstrating its broader social and ideological impacts. By contextualising freedom of expression within democratic values, our work offers a new framework for addressing anti-gender hate speech as a threat to both individual dignity and societal diversity. Through this lens, we highlight how anti-gender hate speech represents not only a breach of individual rights but also a structural challenge to democracy, requiring responses that reflect these dual dimensions. In this book we aim to provide an innovative contribution to both legal scholarship and democratic theory by rethinking the balance between gender equality and freedom of expression as cooperative as well as inherently contextual and inclusive.

After this introduction, a chapter on the theoretical framing follows with the objective to introduce our feminist perspective (Chapter 2). Moreover, we will introduce the theoretical understanding of anti-gender hate speech as a democratic problem counteracting both gender equality and freedom of expression. We will expand on the notions of democracy, gender equality and freedom of expression, and how they are used in the presentation of the problem of anti-gender hate speech, how it is regulated and in the analysis of this. Also, we will introduce the basic principles of criminal legal theory used in our analysis.

In Chapters 3–6, we present the most central regulation on anti-gender hate speech on international, regional and national levels. In regulation we include both policies and law. The regulatory field that we address in Chapter 4 is gender equality, in Chapter 5 freedom of expression, and in Chapter 6 criminal law on hate speech. We will also highlight parts that could include anti-gender hate speech but so far is not.

In the concluding chapter we revisit and rethink anti-gender hate speech in a democratic framing. We end with concluding remarks.

Notes

1 Svea Court of Appeal, judgement in case B 9461–14. The quote, sourced from a comment field beneath a Swedish article on gender equality, contains abusive language and may be distressing for readers. However, reproducing such violent comments is crucial for shedding light on the deeply abusive and violent nature of these interactions, which have become a pervasive part of women's everyday experiences worldwide. This also provides an opportunity to critically examine how online hatred operates and the extent to which it is (or is not) addressed within the framework of criminal law.

2 Södertörn District Court B 6424–20.

3 Despite recent updates to criminal legislation on digital violence, attrition rates for such offences remain exceptionally high. This is partly due to evidentiary challenges, such as the anonymity of offenders and the cross-national complexities of tracing IP addresses. Another significant and troubling aspect of online abuse is its frequent neglect or trivialisation, often dismissed with the argument that 'it was just on the internet', implying that it lacks real-world impact. This tendency is particularly concerning in the context of anti-gender hate speech and other forms of online gender-based violence, where the severity of abuse is already prone to minimisation, resulting in a compounded trivialisation effect.

4 In this book, we will use the terms *freedom of expression* and *freedom of speech* synonymously.

5 We intentionally avoid using the term 'self-censorship', as it implies that the decision not to speak is entirely voluntary. We consider this a problematic assumption and take as a foundational premise that silencing is a structural issue rooted in systemic inequalities.

6 Compensatory measures, such as remedies under tort law, are excluded from the discussion in this book. For those interested, see, e.g., Schultz (2013). We also omit implementation challenges, including difficulties related to anonymity and the inability to share IP addresses across national borders.

References

Literature

Als Research (2015), *Hadytringer og sexism i Norden. Opsamlingsnotat vedrørende Nordisk Ministerråds seminar om hadytringer og sexisme 2.-3. november 2015.* Als Research.

Amnesty International (2018), 'Toxic Twitter: The silencing effect'. www.amnesty.org/en/latest/news/2018/03/online-violence-against-women-chapter-5-5/.

Anderberg, A., Martinsson, D. & Svensson, E. (2022), *Teori och politik. Straffrätt i omvandling*. Iustus Förlag.

Angelari, M. (1993), 'Hate crime statutes: A promising tool for fighting violence against women', *American University Journal of Gender, Social Policy & the Law*, 2(1), 63–105.

Antigona Research Group (2020), *Report on the state of the art on anti-gender hate speech*. https://cris.unibo.it/retrieve/e1dcb335-f518-7715-e053-1705fe0a6cc9/REPORT%20ON%20THE%20STATE%20OF%20THE%20ART%20ON%20ANTI%20GENDER%20HATE%20SPEECH.pdf.

Bakken, T. (2000), 'Liberty and equality through freedom of expression: The human rights questions behind "Hate Crime" laws', *International Journal of Human Rights*, 4(2), 1–12. https://doi.org/10.1080/13642980008406872.

Barker, K. & Jurasz, O. (2019), *Online misogyny as hate crime: A challenge for legal regulation?* 1st ed. Routledge. https://doi.org/10.4324/9780429956805.

Bayer, J. & Bard, J. (2020), *Hate speech and hate crime in the EU and the evaluation of online content regulation approaches*. European Parliament's Policy Department for Citizen's Rights and Constitutional Affairs.

Bladini, M. & NIKK (2017), *Hat och hot på nätet: en kartläggning av den rättsliga regleringen i Norden från ett jämställdhetsperspektiv*. Nordisk information för kunskap om kön, Nordiska ministerrådet.

Bladini, M. (2020), 'Silenced voices. Online violence targeting Women as a Threat to Democracy', *Nordic Journal on Law and Society*, 3(2), 1–42.

Bladini, M. & Svedberg, W. (2020), 'Swedish rape legislation from use of force to voluntariness: Critical reflections from an everyday life perspective', *Bergen Journal of Criminal Law and Criminal Justice*, 8(2), 95–125. https://doi.org/10.15845/bjclcj.v8i2.3241.

BOM (2021), *Näthat och självcensur – det nya normala?* Brottsoffermyndigheten.

Brax, D. (2016), 'Hate speech and the distribution of the costs and benefits of freedom of speech'. In Edström, M., Kenyon, A. T. & Svensson, E-M. (Eds.), *Blurring the lines: Market-driven and democracy-driven freedom of expression*. Nordicom.

Brown, A. & Sinclair, A. (2020), *The politics of hate speech laws*. Routledge.

Carlsson, A. (2024), *Constitutional protection of freedom of expression in the age of social media: A comparative study*. Department of Law, Uppsala University.

Citron, D. K. (2009), 'Law's expressive value in combating cyber gender harassment', *Michigan Law Review*, 108(3), 373–415.

De Giorgi, A., Cavalieri, A. & Feo, F. (2023), *Da leader dell'opposizione a primo ministro: Giorgia Meloni e la questione femminile nella destra radicale italiana*. https://docenti.unimc.it/selena.grimaldi/teaching/2023/28445/files/presentazioni-studenti/presentazione_degiorgi_cavalieri_feo.

De Smedt, T., Jaki, S., Kotzé, E., Saoud, L., Gwóźdź, M., De Pauw, G. & Daelemans, W. (2018), 'Multilingual cross-domain perspectives on online hate speech', *Computational Linguistics & Psycholinguistics Technical Report Series*. University of Antwerpen.

Dunkels, E. (2016), *Nätmobbning, näthat och nätkärlek. Kunskap och strategier för en bättre vardag på nätet*. Gothia Fortbildning AB.

Edström, M. (2016), 'The trolls disappear in the light: Swedish experiences of mediated sexualised hate speech in the aftermath of Behring Breivik', *International Journal for Crime, Justice and Social Democracy*, 5(2), 96–106.

Eriksson, M. (2013), '"Wronged white Men": The performativity of hate in feminist narratives about anti-feminism in Sweden', *NORA: Nordic Journal of Feminist and Gender Research*, 21(4), 249–263.

Eriksson Almgren, T., Ekblad, M. & Sjörén, T. (2017), *Hot mot kvinnliga opinionsbildare*. Kantar SIFO.

Fileborn, B. & Vera-Grey, F. (2017), '"I want to be able to walk the streets without fear": Transforming justice or street harassment', *Feminist Legal Studies*, 25, 203–227.

Flahvin, A. (1995), 'Can legislation prohibiting hate speech be justified in light of free speech principles?' *University of New South Wales Law Journal*, 18(2), 327–340.

Gerstenfeld, P. B. (2017), *Hate crimes causes, controls, and controversies*. Sage Publications.

Giritli Nygren, K., Martinsson, L. & Mulinari, D. (2018), 'Gender equality and beyond: At the crossroads of neoliberalism, anti-gender movements, "European" values, and normative reiterations in the Nordic model', *Social Inclusion*, 6(4), 1–7.

Graff, A. & Korolczuk, E. (2022), *Anti-gender politics in the populist moment*, 1st ed. Routledge. https://doi.org/10.4324/9781003133520.

Granström, G. (2016), 'Hatbrott och kön – en omöjlig kombination?' In Dahlén, M. & Nygren, R (Eds.), *Arbetslinjer och långa linjer: vänbok till Mats Kumlien*. Iustus förlag.

Granström, G., Mellgren, C. & Tiby, E. (2019), *Hatbrott? En introduktion*, 2nd ed. Studentlitteratur AB.

Hagerlid, M. & Granström G. (2023), 'Hate crime investigation and sentencing in Sweden: What have we learned in the past 20 years?' *European Journal on Criminal Policy and Research*. https://link-springer-com.ezproxy.ub.gu.se/article/10.1007/s10610-023-09563-9.

Hellum, A., Ikdahl, I., Blaker Strand, V. & Svensson, E.-M. (2024), *Nordic equality and anti-discrimination laws in the throes of change: Legal developments in Sweden, Finland, Norway, and Iceland*. Taylor & Francis. https://doi.org/10.4324/9781003172840.

Kaati, L., Akrami, N. & Pelzer, B. (2018), *Digitalt hat. Hat och hot mot kommunalpolitiker*. Swedish Association of Local Authorities and Regions (SKL).

Kenyon, A. T., Svensson, E.-M. & Edström, M. (2017), 'Building and sustaining freedom of expression: Considering Sweden', *Nordicom Review*, 38(1), 31–45. https://doi.org/10.1515/nor-2016-0043.

Kováts, E. & Pető, A. (2017), 'Anti-gender discourse in Hungary: A discourse without movement?' In Kuhar, R. & Paternotte, D. (Eds.), *Anti-gender campaigns in Europe: Mobilizing against equality*. Rowman & Littlefield.

Kraus, B. (1993), 'Speech, equality, and harm: Feminist legal perspectives on pornography and hate propaganda', *Off Our Backs*, 23(4), 4–5, 12–21.

Kuhar, R. & Paternotte, D. (2017), *Anti-gender campaigns in Europe: Mobilizing against equality*. Rowman & Littlefield.

Lagiewska, M. (2024), 'Online hate speech under international law'. In Wagner, A. & Marusek, S. (Eds.), *Handbook on cyber hate: The modern cyber* evil. Springer.

Leijonhufvud, M. (2015), *Svensk sexualbrottslag: en framåtsyftande tillbakablick*. Stockholm.

Lilja, M. & Johansson, E. (2018), 'Feminism as power and resistance: An inquiry into different forms of Swedish feminist resistance and anti-genderist reactions', *Social Inclusion*, 6(4), 82–94.

Lundgren, E., Heimer, G., Westerstrand, J. & Kalliokoski, A.-M. (2002), *Captured queen men's violence against women in 'equal' Sweden: A prevalence study.* Brottsoffermyndigheten.

MacKinnon, C. A (1996), *Only words.* Harvard University Press.

McGlynn, C., Rackley, E. & Houghton, R. (2017), 'Beyond "revenge porn": The continuum of image-based sexual abuse', *Feminist Legal Studies*, 25(1), 25–46.

Morini, C. (2024), 'Countering online sexist hate speech in the European legal context: Between present commitment and future challenges', *Questions of International Law*, 104, 17–34.

Mulinari, D. & Neergaard, A. (2017), 'Doing racism, performing femininity: Women in the Sweden democrats'. In Köttig, M., Bitzan, R. & Petö, A. (Eds.), *Gender and far right politics in Europe.* Springer. https://doi.org/10.1007/978-3-319-43533-6_2.

Nielsen, L. B. (2004), *License to harass: Offensive public speech, legal consciousness, and hierarchies of race, gender, and class.* Princeton University Press.

Nordref (2023), *Profiling Nordic perpetrators of gendered online abuse: Who, why and how to curb the harm?* Reykavik.

Norocel, O. C. (2018), 'Antifeminist and "truly liberated": Conservative performances of gender by women politicians in Hungary and Romania', *Politics and Governance*, 6(3), 43–54. https://doi.org/10.17645/pag.v6i3.1417.

Öberg, J. (2024), *The normative foundations for EU criminal justice. Powers, limits and justifications*, Modern Studies in European Law 124. Hart.

Pezzella, F. S. & Fetzer, M. D. (2021), *The measurement of hate crimes in America.* Springer.

Posetti, J., Harrison, J. & Waisbord, S. (2020), 'Online attacks on female journalists are increasingly spilling into the "real" world', *Conversation*, 25 November.

Powell, A., Flynn, A. & Sugiura, L. (2021), *The Palgrave handbook of gendered violence and technology.* Palgrave Macmillan.

Richardson-Self, L. (2018), 'Woman-hating: On misogyny, sexism, and hate speech', *Hypatia*, 33(2), 256–272. https://doi.org/10.1111/hypa.12398.

Richardson-Self, L. (2021), *Hate speech against women online: Concepts and countermeasures.* Rowman & Littlefield.

Schultz, M. (2013), *Näthat – rättigheter och möjligheter.* Karnov Group.

Serughetti, G. (2024), *Potere di altro genere. Donne, femminismi e politica.* Donzelli.

Suler, J. (2004), 'The online disinhibition effect', *Cyber Psychology & Behavior*, 7(3), 321–326.

Sunde, I. M. (2006), *Lov og rett i Cyberspace: Internettkriminalitet og etterforskings metoder.* Fagbokforlaget.

Sundström, M. & Käll, J. (2019), *Kartläggning av förekomsten av könsstereotyp och sexistisk reklam.* The Swedish Equality Ombudsman. www.academia.edu/38463418/Kartl%C3%A4ggning_av_f%C3%B6rekomsten_av_k%C3%B6nsstereotyp_och_sexistisk_reklam-_slutredovisning.

Svensson, E.-M. (1995), 'Vems tryckfrihet – hans, hennes eller hans och hennes?' In *13 Kvinnoperspektiv på rätten.* Nordborg.

Svensson, E.-M. & Bladini, M. (2021), *Report on legal and public policies proposals to address anti-gender hate speech*. http://genha.eu/sites/default/files/pdf/Report%20on%20legal%20and%20public%20policies%20proposals%20-%20copia.pdf.

Svensson, E.-M. & Edström, M. (2014), 'Freedom of expression vs. gender equality: Conflicting values when regulating gender stereotypes in advertising', *Tidsskrift for Rettsvitenskap*, 127(5), 479–511.

Tolstrup Holm, L. (2015), *Kvindelige politikere chikaneres, hånes og trues*. Berlingske. www.berlingske.dk/samfund/kvindelige-politikere-chikaneres-haanes-og-trues (accessed 2024-11-27).

Vickery, J. R. & Everbach, T. (2018), *Mediating misogyny: Gender, technology, and harassment*. Palgrave Macmillan.

Wigerfelt, A. S., Wigerfelt, B. & Dahlstrand, K. (2015), 'Online hate crime: Social norms and the legal system', *Quaestio iuris*, 8(3), 1859–1878. https:/doi.org/10.12957/rqi.2015.

Zempi, I. & Smith, J. (Eds.) (2022), *Misogyny as hate crime*. Routledge.

Court cases

Court of Justice of the European Union (CJEU)

CJEU, judgment of 13 May 2014, Google Spain, C-131/12, EU:C:2014:317.

Swedish court cases

Svea Court of Appeal, judgement in case no. B 9461–14.

Södertörn District Court, judgment in case no. B 6424–20.

Public documents and laws

International (UN)

Convention on the Elimination of All Forms of Discrimination against Women (CEDAW), New York, 18 Dec. 1979, entered into force 3 Sep. 1981. www.ohchr.org/sites/default/files/cedaw.pdf (accessed 2024-10-23).

UN Women (2020), 'The shadow pandemic: Violence against women during Covid-19', www.unwomen.org/en/news/in-focus/in-focus-gender-equality-in-covid-19-response/violence-against-women-during-covid-19 (accessed 2024-11-26).

UNESCO & Broadband Commission (2013). www.unesco.org/en/digital-policy-capacities-inclusion/broadband-commission (accessed 2024-11-27).

United Nations Human Rights Special Procedures (2020), 'Mandate of the Working Group on Discrimination against Women and Girls'. www.ohchr.org/sites/default/files/Documents/Issues/Women/WG/Gender-equality-and-gender-backlash.pdf (accessed 2024-10-23).

International (Council of Europe and EU)

Council of Europe (2011), Convention on Preventing and Combating Violence against Women and Domestic Violence (Istanbul Convention, CETS No. 210, 2011). www.coe.int/en/web/istanbul-convention/text-of-the-convention (accessed 2024-10-23).

Directive (EU) 2024/1385 of the European Parliament and of the Council of 14 May 2024 on Combating Violence against Women and Domestic Violence. https://eur-lex.europa.eu/legal-content/EN/TXT/?uri=OJ%3AL_202401385 (accessed 2024-10-23).

European Commission (2022), COM(2022) 105 final 2022/0066 (COD), Proposal for a Directive of the European Parliament and of the Council on Combating Violence against Women and Domestic Violence. https://eur-lex.europa.eu/legal-content/EN/TXT/PDF/?uri=CELEX:52022PC0105 (accessed 2024-10-23).

European Commission against Racism and Intolerance (ECRI) (2015), ECRI General Policy Recommendation no. 15 on Combating Hate Speech Adopted on 8 December 2015. https://rm.coe.int/ecri-general-policy-recommendation-no-15-on-combating-hate-speech/16808b5b01 (accessed 2024-10-23).

European Institute for Gender Equality (2020), Beijing + 25: The fifth review of the implementation of the Beijing Platform for Action in the EU Member States. https://eige.europa.eu/publications-resources/publications/beijing-25-fifth-review-implementation-beijing-platform-action-eu-member-states (accessed 2024-10-24).

European Institute for Gender Equality (2022), *The EU's evolving legal and policy approaches to gender equality*. EIGE.

InterParliamentary Union (IPU) & Parliamentary Assembly of the Council of Europe (PACE) (Oct. 2018), *Sexism, harassment and violence against women in parliaments own Europe*, Issue Brief.

Sweden

Prop. 2017/18: 177, *En ny sexualbrottslagstiftning byggd på frivillighet*. www.regeringen.se/rattsliga-dokument/proposition/2018/03/prop.-201718177 (accessed 2024-12-16)

Skr. 2016/17: 10, *Makt, mål och myndighet – feministisk politik för en jämställd framtid*. www.regeringen.se/globalassets/regeringen/dokument/socialdepartementet/jamstalldhet/makt-mal-och-myndighet---feministisk-politik-for-ett-jamstallt-samhalle-skr.-2016_17-10.pdf (accessed 2024-11-27).

SOU 2023: 80, *Ett starkare straffrättsligt skydd – mot sexuella kränkningar, bedrägerier i vissa fall och brott med hatmotiv avseende kön*. Betänkande av Utredningen om barns skydd mot sexuella kränkningar samt vissa frågor om brott mot kvinnor och äldre. Elanders Sverige AB. www.regeringen.se/contentassets/e8ccf3b8d03c46db856bc850e8c453dc/ett-starkare-straffrattsligt-skydd--mot-sexuella-krankningar-bedragerier-i-vissa-fall-och-brott-med-hatmotiv-avseende-kon.-sou-202380 (accessed 2024-11-27).

Other sources

Brovall, S. & Christiansen, A. L. (2013), 'Din lille skodfjabbe: Kvindelige journalister hades på nettet'. www.dr.dk/nyheder/kultur/dinlilleskodfjabbekvindeligejournalisterhadespaanettet (accessed 2022-09-06).

2 Theoretical perspective and democratic framework

2.1 Theoretical perspective

We situate ourselves and this book within the legal scholarly field of feminist legal studies. As feminist legal studies emphasise that knowledge is social and *contextual*, recognising the specific context is essential. Various branches of this field have developed over the past 50 years, both in the Nordic region (see, e.g., Svensson 1997; Bladini 2013) and internationally.

Building on this tradition, our focus is the Nordic context, specifically Sweden. This gaze informs our analysis by highlighting how Nordic welfare ambitions and legal frameworks intersect with gendered issues such as online hate speech. The Nordic gaze is shaped by a historically strong tradition of *freedom of expression* in the service of the common good (Kenyon, Svensson & Edström 2017). *Common good* as a criminalisation principle will be discussed further below. It is also influenced by an extensive welfare state with progressive equalising ambitions, often described as 'women-friendly' (Gunnarsson, Svensson & Davies 2007; Hellum et al. 2024). Law is understood as contextual and continuously constructed, inherently interconnected with policy, serving as a tool to structure society and organise everyday life (Svensson 2020). Additionally, we acknowledge the powerful *ideological force of law*, and its role in shaping perceptions and polices (Smart 2002). How an issue is perceived influences its formulation in policy and law, and conversely, how it is formulated in policy and law shapes societal perceptions.

The Nordic context differs from a liberal rights-based context apparent found in other parts of the world, particularly in the Anglo-American tradition (Pylkkänen 2009). In recent years, however, the Nordic model has increasingly aligned with liberal principles (Gustafsson & Svensson 2024). This transformation is also evident in scholarly work, where influences from the internationally dominant liberal tradition on Nordic academia are significant. Nonetheless, there are examples where the Nordic countries influence other parts of the world (see, e.g., Svensson 2025).

The Nordic gaze provides a valuable lens for studying anti-gender hate speech within a democratic framework that emphasises both gender equality and freedom of expression. However, this perspective also reveals troubling

DOI: 10.4324/9781003383062-2

trends, as Nordic characteristics such as extensive welfare ambitions and strong legal frameworks are, in practice, increasingly undermined. We will return to these issues in the forthcoming chapters.

One central presumption of this book is that the *law is gendered* (see, e.g., Svensson 1997; Conaghan 2013; Bladini & Svedberg Andersson 2020; Wettergren, Bladini & Uhnoo 2025). This means that law reflects the unequal power dynamics between men and women. Sexism sustains a patriarchal order, while misogyny, as conceptualised by Manne (2018), enforces it. Misogyny acts as the 'law enforcement' of patriarchy, policing its norms and expectations (p. 78). Its counterpart, *himpathy*, refers to the excessive sympathy extended towards male sexist behaviour, which normalises excusing men's actions – including those of incels[1] – as frustrations or reactions to perceived threats. These dynamics shape social norms beyond formal legal frameworks, influencing everyday life.

Manne (2018) also introduces the concept of *herasure*, which captures the minimisation of women's voices and experiences, particularly when male perspectives are prioritised. Together, himpathy and herasure critique structural biases that prioritise men's feelings while erasing women's perspectives and experiences, thereby perpetuating gender inequality (e.g. Uhnoo, Wettergren & Bladini 2024).

In our analysis, himpathy and herasure are used to examine how and why regulatory means fail to adequately protect women online. The legal system often reflects these dynamics, centring male perspectives in ways that resonate with himpathy. Simultaneously, women's experiences are diminished, treated as isolated incidents rather than systemic patterns, aligning with herasure. Criminal law generally overlooks systemic patterns of gender-based harm, with notable exceptions such as aggravated violations of women's integrity, which explicitly acknowledge such patterns (Andersson 2004, 2011; Burman 2007). This marginalisation mirrors the narrative of *The God of Small Things* (Roy 1997), where everyday injustices are obscured in favour of dominant narratives.

The *everyday life perspective*, developed by Dorothy Smith in 1987 (2012), emphasises grounding legal analysis in lived experiences rather than abstract notions. MacKinnon (2016) critiques the legal system's failure to reflect social realities, creating barriers in court, while Naffine (2002) highlights how rape harm is often abstracted rather than rooted in women's everyday experiences. Both scholars argue that legal frameworks must address the structural biases that perpetuate gender inequality.

Building on this, Svedberg (2013) further developed everyday life as an analytical concept in legal studies. Applying this perspective, Bladini and Svedberg Andersson (2020) show how situational and relational factors shape autonomy. They critique Swedish rape legislation, revealing a male-oriented rationale in preparatory works and calling for deeper examination of voluntariness. Similarly, Andersson (2004, 2011) and Burman (2007) highlight gaps in criminal law's recognition of systemic gender-based harm, with notable exceptions like aggravated violations of women's integrity. These perspectives collectively argue for legal frameworks that centre women's lived realities and address structural inequalities, a key perspective in this book.

We draw on Kelly's (1988) *continuum of sexual violence* as a framework to analyse how diverse forms of harassment and abuse against women are interconnected. This continuum is understood in at least two ways. First, it captures a continuous series of actions or events that cannot be easily distinguished (Kelly 1988, 76). Second, it identifies a 'basic common character' – abuse, coercion, intimidation, intrusion, threat, and force – that underpins and links otherwise disparate phenomena. By using this framework, we can contextualise women's experiences of violence as systemic rather than isolated, highlighting how gender inequality is perpetuated through various forms of control.

Kelly's concept of the *continuum of violence* has been expanded and elaborated by other scholars. In the Nordic context, Lundgren et al. (2002) applied it in a prevalence study of men's violence against women in Sweden. They described the concept as linking serious acts of violence with less overt or criminalised behaviours, emphasising that all forms of gender-related violence are serious and rejecting hierarchical distinctions between them. In an online context, the continuum has been further developed by McGlynn, Rackley and Houghton (2017) and Bladini (2020).

Lundgren's work also introduced the concept of the *normalisation of violence*, which had a significant impact on Swedish gender equality policy in the 1990s. This theory underpinned legislative changes, such as the introduction of the crime of gross violation of a woman's peace (Prop. 1997/98: 55). Lundgren argued that violent relationships involve a gradual shifting of boundaries, where acts of violence take on new meanings over time. She highlighted *controlling behaviour* as a form of violence that impacts women's personal space and autonomy, including actions like jealousy, isolation from friends and family, and financial control. Such behaviours, while not always physical, can severely undermine women's integrity and self-esteem (Lundgren et al. 2002).

The continuum of violence has also been illustrated through the *pyramid of violence* (Franzén & Gottzén 2020), which emphasises the interconnectedness of less severe and more severe forms of violence. This perspective is reflected in Swedish gender equality policy, particularly in the sub-goal focusing on the elimination of violence (Regeringskansliet 2016).[2]

The *fragmentation* of anti-gender hate speech across global, regional, and national jurisdictions – and its classifications within multiple legal fields – presents both a challenge and a starting point for this study. Anti-gender hate speech is situated within gender equality as it constitutes discrimination and violence against women, making it an obstacle to achieving gender equality (Barker & Jurasz 2020). It is also linked to freedom of expression as a form of speech and to criminal law as a frequently proposed regulatory mechanism.

This complexity, which will be evident in Chapter 4-6, underscores the need for a cohesive analytical framework.

This book addresses the fragmentation by combining concepts and theories that describe, explain, and explore anti-gender hate speech as a legal and social phenomenon. The feminist legal theoretical framework and democratic framing employed here enable a more cohesive analysis of anti-gender hate speech than previous research has achieved.

In the following, we provide an overview of anti-gender hate speech as a phenomenon rooted in everyday life, inherently gendered, and thus a barrier to gender equality. We also examine its relationship to democracy, specifically its foundational elements of gender equality and freedom of expression and its implications for fundamental principles of criminalisation.

More specifically, we explore how anti-gender hate speech functions as gender stereotypical and as a form of violence against women, undermining gender equality. We also analyse how it may silence women, thereby restricting freedom of expression. Additionally, we assess how anti-gender hate speech may constitute *harm* and a *public wrong*, potentially subject to criminalisation. However, consistent with the *principle of proportionality* and *ultima ratio*, criminal law should be the last resort.

Three regulative fields are thus central to this study: gender equality, freedom of expression, and criminal law.

2.2 Defining anti-gender hate speech

Starting with the definition of hate speech, it is essential to note that there is no universal or legal definition of the phenomenon. There is, however, a growing body of academics', legal experts' and policymakers' contributions to how to define it, even if a consensus is not reached. The definitions also vary between governmental institutions such as the UN, the Council of Europe, EU and national parliaments and policymakers.

In a UN context, the first human rights instrument prohibiting certain 'propagation' and 'promotion of ideas' was the International Convention on the Elimination of All Forms of Racial Discrimination (ICERD) in 1965, if endorsed by public authorities or institutions concerning racial superiority or racial discrimination. Hate speech typically refers to expressions aimed at degrading, demeaning, or inciting hatred or violence against individuals or groups based on their identity. It can take various forms, including verbal insults, online harassment, physical violence, and hate crimes. While hate speech causes harm to its direct targets, it also affects society at large by fostering a climate of fear and intolerance. Targeting individuals based on inherent characteristics such as race, religion, or gender, hate speech poses a threat to social harmony (Lagiewska 2024). We argue that anti-gender hate speech threatens democracy, in addition to being a threat to social harmony.

According to the UN hate speech is defined as 'any kind of communication in speech, writing or behaviour, that attacks or uses pejorative or discriminatory language with reference to a person or a group on the basis of who they are, in other words, based on their religion, ethnicity, nationality, race, colour, descent, gender or other identity factor' (United Nations n.d.b). Notably is that gender is included on this definition.

There are both broad and narrow definitions (Lagiewska 2024) in various aspects, especially concerning which kind of *speech and actions* are included and which targeted individuals and groups that are recognised as exposed to hate speech and thus, included in the definition.

In the research project behind this book, GENHA, we elaborated on three modalities, spanning from a narrow to a broad form. These are anti-gender hate speech in *the narrow sense*, in *the broad sense* and hate speech *potential* (Fejös & Zentai 2021).

The targets of anti-gender hate speech were divided into three distinctive and intersecting categories; (1) individual and groups of women (expressed as anti-women's rights and sexism) (2) individuals and groups defined by their sexual orientation, identity and expression (expressed as anti-LGBTQI+ and homophobia), and (3) ideologies of gender equality, feminism and all equal values (expressed as anti-genderism; Fejös & Zentai 2021: 12).

Fejös and Zentai (2021) identify three modalities of hate speech. Hate speech in the narrow sense (HSN) involves explicit incitement to physical violence, such as assault or rape, targeting individuals or groups like women, LGBTQI persons, and feminist activists. Hate speech in the broad sense (HSB) employs degrading language aimed at denying social membership and political belonging to those advocating for gender equality, sexual identity rights, and minority protections. The third modality, hate speech potential (HSP), includes discourse around topics such as gender, family, and sexuality, reinforcing essentialist and hierarchical gender roles while rejecting relationships outside of conservative heterosexual norms.

A distinction is made between *explicit hate speech*, which overtly expresses intent, and *implicit hate speech*, which relies on subtler language with less obvious intentions. While HSN typically includes explicit calls to action, both HSB and HSP can manifest in explicit or implicit forms. The intensity of hate speech lies not in its linguistic expression but in its communicative function and ideological framework.

These definitions are revisited throughout the book, drawing on and extending the ECRI definition and GENHA framework. The primary focus is on *anti-gender hate speech*, targeting women (target 1) and ideological attacks on principles of gender equality and minority rights (target 3). This focus addresses a gap in legal scholarship and regulation, both internationally and nationally, in these areas.

These modalities reflect a spectrum of violence, cf. continuum of violence, where explicit incitement (HSN) represents its most overt form, while the subtler expressions of HSB and HSP sustain structural violence and normalise discrimination. HSP, in particular, serves to legitimise the progression from implicit to explicit forms of violence, illustrating the continuum's fluidity and interconnectedness.

2.3 Anti-gender hate speech: A democratic problem

Anti-gender hate speech is increasingly perceived as a democratic problem, with negative consequences for democracy. It is discriminatory and counteracts the goal of gender equality and it may lead to the silencing of certain voices. Much of the political discussions today take place online, which not only demands access to technical facilities but also a friendly and including climate to encourage everyone to take part. If women are exposed to hate speech and as a consequence are deliberately (or even undeliberate) silenced, it is truly a democratic problem. To expand on this argument a brief exploration of the notion of democracy and its basic components is urgent. Of specific importance here is to identify the principles that are or might be affected by anti-gender hate speech.

2.3.1 What is democracy and how is it justified?

The perception of democracy comes in many versions, elaborated upon below. How democracy is talked about impact the implementation of it. We suggest that the discourse on democracy is important for the way anti-gender hate speech is dealt with.

Democracy as a concept is both political, an ideal and ideology, and analytical, used to evaluate various states level of democracy around the world. Politically it is a word of honour, something to strive for, at least in most parts of the world. The ideal is mirrored by an ideology explicitly expressed by states and other public bodies and implicitly forming the organisation of society, politics and legislation.

The analytical comparison of the world's democracies of todays', using V-Dem data and four regime categories (Lürhmann, Tannenberg & Lindberg 2018; Varieties of Democracy, V-dem), divides between two kinds of democracy, electoral and liberal (opposed to the non-democratic regimes closed autocracy and electoral autocracy). Only a minority of the world's countries are considered to be a democracy in its most comprehensive form, and generally speaking democracy is even declining, and autocracy increases (Varieties of Democracy, V-dem). According to the Democracy Index 2023 by the Economist Intelligence Unit (2006–2023) the countries ranking high are found in the western world (i.e. Europe, the American continent, Australia, India and South Africa). Democracy as in those countries requires not only free and fair elections, but also for instance that the population participate in politics.

A minority of the world's countries are considered being on the highest level of democracies, liberal democracies according to V-dem. Included in this category are the Nordic countries (Denmark, Finland, Iceland, Norway and Sweden), several other European countries and the USA, slightly different from the characterisation by the Economist Intelligence Unit. Spain has undergone a transformation from a closed autocracy to a liberal democracy since 1972 and Italy has a question mark if it is liberal or just electoral. The representative element is, if not complemented by other elements, in focus for an electoral democracy, while a liberal democracy consists of more core principles than the electoral, such as the following.

The dataset of V-Dem identifies several core principles of democracy, among them electoral, liberal, participatory, egalitarian and deliberative, and V-Dem collects data to measure these principles.

The electoral principle of democracy captures the extent to which regimes hold clean, free and fair elections, their actual freedom of expression, alternative sources of information and association, as well as male and female suffrage and the degree to which government policy is vested in elected political officials. Relevant here is the importance given to freedom of expression. *The liberal principle of democracy* embodies the importance of strong rule of law and constitutionally protected civil liberties, independent judiciary and strong parliament that can hold the executive to account and limit its powers. Here, the responsibility of an active state is relevant.

The *participatory principle of democracy* emphasises active participation by citizens in all political processes, electoral and non-electoral. This principle prefers direct rule by citizens as practicable. Together with the *egalitarian principle of democracy* measuring to what extent all social groups enjoy equal capabilities to participate in the political arena, these two core principles are highly relevant. As anti-gender hate speech may have the effect that certain individuals and groups are silenced, this is obviously contradictory to active participation on equal terms. The latter relies on the idea that democracy is a system of rule 'by the people' where citizens participate in various ways, such as making informed voting decisions, expressing opinions, demonstrating, running for office or influencing policymaking in other ways. The egalitarian principle of democracy is fundamentally related to political participation, as systematic inequalities in the rights and resources of citizens of specific social groups limit capabilities to participate in the political and governing processes. Therefore, a more equal distribution of resources across groups results in political equality and hence democracy.

The *deliberative principle of democracy* has to do with the process by which decisions are reached in polity. A deliberative process is one in which public reasoning, focused on the common good, motivates political decisions – as contrasted with emotional appeals, solidary attachments, parochial interests or coercion. According to this principle, democracy requires more than an aggregation of existing preferences. There should also be respectful dialogue at all levels – from preference formation to final decision – among informed and competent participants who are open to persuasion. What is also notable here is the focus on the common good.

As we can see, anti-gender hate speech might counteract several of the principles above. Freedom of expression will be elaborated below. The egalitarian principle addresses the importance of participation of the citizens in democracy. If citizens are to be able to make informed voting decisions, expressing opinions, demonstrating, running for office or influencing policymaking in other ways it is important with a broad inflow of opinions, ideas etc. If some voices are silenced it limits the ability to make informed decisions. Systematic inequalities in the rights and resources of citizens of specific social groups limit capabilities to participate in the political and governing processes. Therefore, a more equal distribution of resources across groups results in political equality and hence democracy.

The deliberative principle requires public reasoning, focus on common good, motivated political decisions, and more than an aggregation of existing preferences. There should also be respectful dialogue at all levels – from preference formation to final decision – among informed and competent participants who are open to persuasion. Such an aim is contrasted with emotional appeals, solidary attachments, parochial interests or coercion. Anti-gender hate speech triggers emotions, hate and coercion and not public reasoning, nor focus on common good or motivated political decisions.

The core principles highlighted by V-dem can be compared with the notion of democracy in a Swedish context. The self-image of Swedish democracy, confirmed in international evaluations as will be elaborated below, is quite positive, the ideal is supposed to be clear and stable and embraced by everyone. A commission of inquiry on power and democracy in the late 1980s (SOU 1990: 44), declared the Swedish ideal as tightened to the idea of sovereignty of the people (*folksuveränitet*), and to everybody's participation in the society's decision processes and in opinion formation. It is an everyday practice version of democracy, performed in politics, unions and in the neighbourhood and working places, etc. The ideal is also tightened to everybody's equal value. From the equality principle derives the demand that everybody should have the same ability to influence their living conditions and the development of all areas of society, not only formally but also de facto. Such ability presupposes an even distribution of resources, economic, organisational, and power resources, knowledge and competences, self-confidence and contact with influential persons. Inequalities and a sense of powerlessness hazard the very foundation of democracy and its basic prerequisite solidarity among the citizens.

The ideal seems to contain several of the core principles pointed at by V-dem, but in addition it is characterised by a societal-oriented tradition. The common interest, the population's supposed collective identity and the individual's responsibility for others in addition to responsibility for oneself, have been at the core. Over time, a more individual-oriented perception of democracy, according to which a sovereign individual is expected to be responsible for itself, has emerged. Irrespective of this, a basic thought is that everyone should be counted as alike regarding decisions about how society shall be governed. Also, there is an indissoluble connection between democracy and power (SOU 1990: 44, 17).

Power was in the Commission from 1990 elaborated as a thick concept. In the third chapter concerning the gender system, power was defined as taking place on somebody else's behalf. This meaning of power is important to understand how anti-gender hate speech is an action of power. With such an understanding it becomes clear that responsibility must be taken in relation to others, to claim space means that other's space may be restricted. And if the claim is combined with hateful content the restricting effect becomes even worse.

Over time, the discourse on democracy in Sweden as elsewhere has undergone a transformation. At the same time as the individual-oriented understanding has been strengthened, the principle of gender equality, emphasising the importance of equally distributed resources of both material and immaterial kind, has been devalued. And the talk about democracy has been narrowed, the Swedish government of today declares on its website democracy to be representative (Vad är demokrati?). Also, the talk about rule of law is increasing, emphasising formal rights on behalf of welfare measures securing equal access to and capabilities to participate in democracy. The government's declaration may indicate a narrowing down of the most basic meaning of democracy, to a perception consisting of two components, majority rule and individual rights and freedoms.

Other statements however counteract this picture. The most recent commission on democracy (SOU 2022: 28), emphasises participation and equal influence. This seems to confirm previously declarations of Swedish democracy as a participatory democracy with deliberative qualities (SOU 2000: 1), alternatively as emphasising equal influence, participation and representation (SOU 2016: 5). Such a democracy model focuses on conversation (debate) and the fundamental importance of open-minded and rational argumentation. However, if compared with how anti-gender hate speech has been handled so far, a reluctance to combat it and not in line with how hate speech based on ethnicity and sexual orientation, makes it clear that the rhetoric about democracy is not implemented when the target group is women. Sweden as a role model when it comes to gender equality (see, e.g., Svensson 2025) has its blind spots, which will be further elaborated in Chapter 4.

2.4 Gender equality

In this section we focus on gender equality and how anti-gender hate speech might be an obstacle to the achievement of this political and legal goal and principle. The two aspects increasingly referred to are that anti-gender hate speech is gender stereotypical and constitute gender-based violence.

Gender equality is an essential element of democracy, as shown in the section on democracy above. It is an ideal and a goal for the global society, widely declared in legal instruments, in political agendas and agreements. As Kate Malleson declared in 2003, 'it is now so widely accepted that the goal of gender equality in public life generally, and the judiciary specifically, is an unqualified good, that to ask the question why this is necessary seems redundant if not perverse'. At the same time, there are groups in society that questions the ideal, for instance the anti-gender movements mentioned in Chapter 1. Thus, it is plausible to say that it is a contested ideal which is relevant to be aware of when addressing anti-gender hate speech.

The meaning of gender equality is shifting. It may be understood in terms of formal equal rights (as in the wording of the UN Declaration), as substantive in the meaning of equal opportunities or as transformative as in shared power and responsibility between men and women, improving of women's rights and as the empowerment of women and girls. It can be used interchangeably with the concept *equal rights of men and women*, which primarily is used in legal instruments, while gender equality most often is used in political documents (Svensson 2021). As we address both law and policies on anti-gender hate speech, we use gender equality throughout the text. Most often the two concepts indicate the same meaning. For example, the European Institute for Gender Equality (EIGE) defines gender equality as 'equal rights (sometimes expressed as treatments), responsibilities and opportunities of women and men and girls and boys' not dependent on sex at birth. It implies that interests, needs, and priorities of women and men should be considered, recognising the diversity of different groups of women and men without meaning that women and men should become the same. Gender equality is not, according to EIGE, a 'women's issue' but should concern and fully engage men. It is seen as a human rights issue and a precondition for, and indicator of, sustainable people-centred development (EIGE 2024).

Gender equality relates to the concept equality (Fredman 2022) but has also its specific genealogic story, to some extent different in various context (for the Nordic context, see Pylkkänen 2009 and Hellum et al. 2024; for the Anglo-American context see Fredman 2022). What is common are the various ways how the goals, expressed as political values and legal principles are perceived, and how this relates to which measures are considered proper, possible and proportionate to promote the principles. Questions of who should be equal to whom and in what respect remain, but the fundamental principles of equality and gender equality can be interpreted as *formal, substantive or transformative* based on perceptions of how equality should be achieved. Formal equality (de jure equality) means full equality before the law and protection against discrimination. Substantive equality (de facto equality or equality of outcome) requires appropriate measures be taken, including at times temporary special measures (Svensson 2021). Transformative equality addresses systemic and structural discrimination that may be embedded in laws (and policies) intended to reconsider and transform stereotypes and cultural practices and overcome structural discrimination (Holtmaat 2013). Most jurisdictions and legal instruments embrace a combination of formal and substantive equality, while some instruments such as CEDAW have a transformative approach, at least to some extent (Hellum & Aasen 2013). Political agendas are more likely to embrace elements of transformation (Svensson 2021). This is notable also in measures to combat anti-gender hate speech.

Also, the meaning of the concept of equality differs. Sandra Fredman (2022) has stated that 'equality as an ideal shines brightly in the galaxy of liberal aspirations. It is also a central pillar of international and domestic human rights instruments. Yet the more closely we examine it, the more its meaning shifts'. According to UN gender equality was made part of international human rights law by the Universal Declaration of Human Rights, adopted by the UN General Assembly on 10 December 1948, although in the wordings of equal rights (United Nations n.d.a). The universal declaration recognised, 'All human beings are born free and equal in dignity and rights' and that 'everyone is entitled to all the rights and freedoms set forth in this Declaration, without distinction of any kind, such as race, colour, sex, language, religion ... birth or other status'. In Chapter 4 the regulation on gender equality will be further elaborated. What is highlighted here are the presumptions for gender equality and why anti-gender hate speech is to be understood as an obstacle to achieve the goal.

There are various tools to achieve gender equality (Hellum et al. 2024; Svensson & Gunnarsson 2012) but the main legal tool is the implementation of the non-discrimination principle. This is also declared in the UN Declaration mentioned above (everyone is entitled to all the rights and freedoms ... without distinction of any kind). The non-discrimination principle has been elaborated and further developed in policies and legal instruments over time. The expectations on states and other governmental bodies to take action to eliminate discrimination of women have increased and according to the main human right instrument promoting women's rights, the dynamic instrument CEDAW, the states are obliged to take all appropriate measures to eliminate discrimination against women.

Gender equality is an essential element in a democracy. For instance, the Swedish gender equality goal clearly connects it to democracy and moreover, it also connects power to violence (Gender Equality Policy in Sweden 2024). The main gender equality goal, that everyone shall have the same power to influence society and their own life, is divided into several sub-goals that are interrelated and mutually influencing each other. One goal is the elimination of gendered violence, another is equal power to take part in the formation of society, in political and economic life. To secure women from being exposed to violence it is necessary to guarantee women taking place in political and economic life.

Anti-gender hate speech targets someone on the ground of sex/gender. Such speech may be based on stereotypes which devaluate women and may lead to violence. Stereotypes may affect everyone; however, they have often a particularly egregious effect on women.

> Stereotypes degrade women when they assign them to subservient roles in society and devalue their attributes and characteristics. Prejudices about women's inferiority and their stereotyped roles generate disrespect and devaluation of women in all sectors of society. Women themselves may be socially conditioned to absorb negative stereotypes about themselves, and to fulfill the subordinate, passive role they consider appropriate to their status. When societies fail to recognize and eliminate such prejudices and theory associated stereotypes, that failure exacerbates a climate of impunity with respect to violations of women's rights. The climate of impunity enables prejudices and wrongful gender stereotypes to fester, causing further devaluation of women.
>
> (Cook & Cusack 2010: 1)

Stereotypes are interpreted within the CEDAW framing, by the Committee, as a form of discrimination against women (General Recommendation no. 25). It's also declared that gender-based stereotypes affect women not only through individual acts by individuals but also in law, and legal and societal structures and institutions. And, following being a party to the convention, the states are obliged to (among other things) address prevailing gender relations and the persistence of gender-based stereotypes that affect women not only through individual acts by individuals but also in law, and legal and societal structures and institutions.

Anti-gender hate speech is thus increasingly declared as violence against women and as such discriminatory. Gender-based violence is defined, by the CEDAW Committee (General Recommendation no. 35) as violence that is directed against a woman because she is a woman or that affects women disproportionately. It includes acts that inflict physical, mental or sexual harm or suffering, threats of such acts, coercion and other deprivations of liberty. Gender-based violence may breach specific provisions of the Convention, regardless of whether those provisions expressly mention violence. The violence takes multiple forms, including acts or omissions intended or likely to cause or result in death or physical, sexual, psychological or economic harm or suffering to women, threats of such acts, harassment, coercion and arbitrary deprivation of liberty. Gender-based violence against women is affected and often exacerbated by cultural, economic, ideological, technological, political, religious, social and environmental factors.

CEDAW connects various forms in the violence concept. We will further connect this view to the concepts of the continuum of violence framework, the normalisation of violence and the pyramid of violence. These concepts will be used as tools to understand and analyse online anti-gender hate speech as connected to other forms of gendered violence, and to explore the potential impact for policy and law, as they are discursive and forms our way to perceive the speech at stake. We suggest, in line with McGlynn, Rackley and Houghthon (2017) who have developed the continuum of violence into the concept *the continuum of image-based sexual abuse*, that this is urgent due to advances in technology. The technological development facilitates an increased use of and consequences of online anti-gender hate speech, and persons who are targeted or react have difficulties to defend themselves from the speech also in social media, which dissolves the boundary between the private and the public sphere.

To abridge to next section, we are convinced that understanding anti-gender hate speech as something that goes beyond the individual and the group levels, including also the discursive level, which in this context means ideas on a symbolic and societal level, connects the phenomenon to democracy and in more detail freedom of expression. Democracy requires that everyone has the same right, possibility and power to form society and one's own life. The responsibility to secure such a practice is not only a matter for individuals but also for the state and other governing bodies. This goes well together with the perception of freedom of speech as two-folded, not only as a freedom from interventions in form of censorship, but also as guaranteeing *a diversity of voices*. Measures to safeguard a diversity of voices are necessary to foster a democratic society (Kenyon, Svensson & Edström 2017).

2.5 Freedom of expression

We approach anti-gender hate speech as a democratic problem of general character and not only or even mainly as a problem for those who are exposed to this kind of speech. When certain individuals' or groups' possibilities to participate in conversations online are undermined and their voices silenced as a result of them being exposed to anti-gender hate speech, the result is a one-sided and a non-diverse debate. Democracy, generally perceived as an ideal of inclusion and something to strive for, is not achieved if not all voices have access to raise their voices and to be heard. In this chapter we will elaborate upon the democratic framework forming the backdrop of anti-gender hate speech. Anti-gender hate speech may be contradictory to democracy.

2.5.1 The role of freedom of expression in a democratic society: Promoting a diversity of voices

Freedom of expression is a basic element in a democracy. According to evaluations of democracies, such as the one presented above and performed by V-Dem, this element is included in the narrowest form of democracy, the electoral. Most constitutions and international human rights conventions, such as for example ECHR, declare everyone's right to freedom of expression. Thus, the freedom is formulated as an individual right to express oneself. If seen primarily as an individual right, it follows that not restricting the individual from expressing what he or she want, is the way to safeguard the right. In many parts of the world freedom of expression is perceived in this way, as requiring guarantees against state intervention, expressed as 'negative free speech' (Kenyon 2021). This approach is specifically predominant in countries where liberal and libertarian ideologies are predominant (Carlsson 2024).

However, freedom of expression is much more than this. It is commonly valued for multiple reasons: it is said to aid in discovering truth or developing knowledge, to serve people's interest in self-development or autonomy, and to be necessary for democratic forms of self-government (Petäjä 2006). The ways in which countries protect and promote freedom of expression differ greatly. However, within formally democratic constitutional systems free speech can be understood to have two basic aspects: non-censorship and diversity of voices (e.g. Lichtenberg 1990). What we call democratic framing (or rationality) implies that freedom of expression is much more than an individual right to express oneself. It is seen as a basic prerequisite for democracy together with the important right to information.[3] The basic justification of freedom of expression is that it serves democracy, or the common good (Kenyon, Svensson & Edström 2017; Petäjä 2006). This way of perceiving freedom of expression and the link between freedom of expression and democracy, is central to the Nordic countries (Kenyon, Svensson & Edström 2017).

2.5.2 Justifying freedom of expression

There are various theories justifying the protection of freedom of expression (or speech). Kenyon, Svensson and Edström (2017) point out three, an aid in discovering truth or developing knowledge, to serve people's interest in self-development or autonomy, and to be necessary for democratic forms of self-government (Kenyon, Svensson & Edström 2017). In her thesis, Anni Carlsson argues it is essential to know why free speech is worth protecting, to avoid the risk of ad hoc and less principled responses to arguments of limiting free speech, or, as we would prefer to frame it, to balance free speech to other values. 'It can make it more difficult for a democratic society to defend itself against undemocratic forces if something as essential for democracy as freedom of expression is just taken for granted without an understanding of what in fact makes it valuable' (Carlsson 2024, 65, with reference to Petäjä 2006). In the age of social media, it is even more relevant to have a clear picture of what it is we actually protect, due to the contours of the right must be established in a novel technological context (Carlsson 2024, 66). Online gender-based hate speech do certainly proliferate in this openly accessible technological context, which requires thoroughly considerations when trying to do something about it.

Carlsson takes on the endeavour to analyse the constitutional protection of freedom of expression on social media in the USA, Germany and Sweden within the framework of European law (ECHR and EU law), presents and analyses the most central justifications of the protection of freedom of expression. The so-called classical theories are according to her, search for truth, democratic self-government, autonomy and tolerance. The first three are comparable to the ones pointed out by Kenyon, Svensson and Edström (2017). Carlsson (2024) in addition presents a relational theory of free speech based on the republican notion of freedom as non-domination.

The dominance of English and American theories is quite obvious. There are, however, other ways to justify freedom of expression. The Swedish political scientist Ulf Petäjä (2006) contributes to the theories of free speech by pointing at the common value in all the previous arguments, the reliable communication process. We will in the following in short present the various arguments, and their connection to some important distinctions which we will use in the analysis in Chapter 4. The distinctions are negative and republican freedom which are connected to non-interference and non-domination respectively, unhindered and protected free speech, public and private power and negative and positive free speech related to a passive and an active state respectively.

According to the 19th-century liberal philosopher Mill (*On Liberty* 1859), freedom of expression is important due to its centrality as a means for finding the truth. Accepted facts and received opinions might, under the truth theory, be tested, scrutinised and cross-examined which might lead to more or better truth. Holmes used the metaphor of the marketplace of ideas to conceptualise the search for truth coming with a free market-like competition between ideas, where the truth ultimately appears as a winner (Carlsson 2024, 68). With this theory, freedom of expression is synonymous with non-interference, and with negative freedom.

The democratic self-government means, advocated by Meiklejohn, that the purpose of freedom of expression is to make citizens of a democratic society capable of governing themselves. All citizens must therefore understand the issues which bear upon our common life, which allows or even requires the state to take an active role in enlarging and enriching free speech through regulation (Carlsson 2024, 68). With help of this democratic theory, it can be argued that the state must regulate mass media to counteract media concentration and to promote public interest requirements on media and creating access rights as well as diversity of voices. The Swedish regulation of mass media and public service is one example of such regulations. Another proponent of this theory is Habermas, focusing on public discourse and deliberative democracy. Habermas puts his trust in the communicative rationality, relying on discourse ethics, norms for rational conversation and processes to safeguard such rationality. Interesting is that Sweden, when presenting its democracy model in 2000, declared it to be deliberative (SOU 2000: 1).

The autonomy argument was to start with basically that individuals should be protected from state interference. However, its proponent Scanlon later revised his argument and allowed for more state interference in order to promote a good expressive environment. For example, the state might suppress certain forms of expression, such as fraudulent advertising. And, moreover, Scanlon has also made it clear that autonomy perhaps is not the most important value underlying the protection of freedom of expression (Carlsson 2024, 71–72).

Freedom of expression has also been justified as a means for promoting tolerance in society, developed in depth by Bollinger (1986). He sees the area of speech 'as an appropriate arena for members of society to practice tolerance. Requiring them to tolerate different types of expression, even hateful ones, trains their ability to be tolerant in other areas of social interaction too' (Carlsson 2024, 73). The goal of free speech is thus seen as developing particular intellectual attitudes, capacity of mind and a way of thinking.

The proponents of the relational theory of free speech based on the republican notion of freedom as non-domination, Bonotti and Seglow, claim that the classic theories do not fulfil the criteria that an adequate theory of free speech should meet. Bonotti and Seglow identify four necessary criteria: specialness, stringency, no internal balancing and opportunities. The first is that it must be possible to identify why freedom of expression is special and should be distinguished from liberty in general. Second, it must be clear why some categories of speech are regarded as particularly valuable and granted more stringent protection. This is the case in, for example, Swedish jurisdiction, in which 'commercial messages' have a lower degree of protection (Kenyon, Svensson & Edström 2017; Svensson 2016) in contrast to what is the case in American context (where *commercial speech* is as protected as *political speech*). Inspired by the American context, and using the concept of commercial speech, some advocates from advertisement industry have argued to strengthen the protection for commercial messages in the Swedish context (Svensson & Edström 2014: 503–504, 2016; Edström & Svensson 2016).

The third criteria, no internal balancing, means that it should not be possible to use the value justifying freedom of expression to silence speech. And the fourth and last criteria, the substantive opportunities of citizens to speak must be safeguarded, not only the formal right. Bonotti and Seglow identify speech as a form of recognition. Thus, for example hate speech and fake news may be limited with this relational view (Carlsson 2024, 75–77).

The contribution by Petäjä diverges from the above-mentioned justifications. He has analysed them all with the aim to find an underlying shared common value. He finds almost all arguments consequentialist, which means that they justify freedom of expression as a means for achieving some other good. He notes all of the arguments are anchored in promoting common rather than individual interests. Moreover, they mainly focus on protecting the free speech rights of the audience rather than those of the speakers. On the basis of these conclusions Petäjä means that it is possible to regard freedom of expression from two distinct ideal-typical positions, as a collective good or as an individual right. If regarded as a collective good, freedom of expression is justified on consequentialist grounds, promoting common interest and focused primarily on the interest of the audience. If perceived as an individual right, it is justified on non-consequentialist ground seen as promoting individual interests and focused primarily on the interest of the speaker. Petäjä also argues that freedom of expression should be seen as a method with the aim to produce a reliable communication process in public communication. And, even if he, according to Carlsson (2024, 74), means that all the above-mentioned theories share the value of the reliable communicative process, we consider his thoughts highly accurate for the Swedish context. This context is characterised by its pragmatic view on law and by its extensive constitutional protection of freedom of expression explicitly based on the common good position. In addition, media has also constitutional protection as a mechanism for scrutinising the exercise of power (Kenyon, Svensson & Edström 2017). Kenyon, Svensson and Edström (2017) call this position 'the democratic rationale for free speech'. Such approach takes it beyond a bare liberty against government action. Free speech includes obligations for a certain 'state of affairs' to be sought. Alexy and Rivers (2010) use the concept of a state of affairs in relation to broadcasting freedom (and other constitutional rights in Germany), and it appears useful to adopt here. Free speech involves not just what the state should refrain from doing, but also what the state and others should do to support the environment for speech (Kenyon 2014, 2016; Karppinen 2016). The changing and uncertain media environment may increase the challenges for state action to support diverse speech, but it does not remove the value of such efforts (Kenyon, Svensson & Edström 2017).

In the Nordic countries, the state is clearly expected to be active in guaranteeing both a wide freedom of expression and diversity when it comes to both content and media providers (Kenyon, Svensson & Edström 2017; Syvertsen et al. 2014). Freedom of expression is perceived as a positive right and the extensive constitutional system, especially prevalent in Sweden, is a combination of provisions guaranteeing independent media and enabling the public diversity, 'positive free speech' (Kenyon 2021). Media has a prominent role in and for democracy, even though the technical development has facilitated individual's access to mediated speech in social media and internet forum. Individual access to the internet worldwide is seen as a promotion of democracy according to one of the Swedish commissions on power (SOU 2000: 1). At the same time individual access to dissemination of opinions etc. might also be a risk. Contrary to traditional media produced by professional journalists, individuals do not always adhere to the responsibility that follows with the use of expression. The responsibility is in Sweden partly legally regulated, as misuse of freedom of expression in the constitutions guaranteeing freedom of expression and, for professionals, in various Code of conducts. From start, when freedom of expression was first expressed in a constitutional act in Sweden in the late 18th century, it was the right to publish that was protected not the right to speak otherwise. The media, or from the start the press, has been the main medium for expression (Carlsson 2016). Thus, it was the press that was given the central role in freedom of expression and protected in constitutional acts. Only quite recently, in the 1970s, the individual right to express oneself became constitutionally protected. Still, especially in Sweden, the press and other media has an extensive protection while the individual right to express oneself is less protected. What is more, all kinds of expressions are not considered equally worthy of protection. There are expressions that fall outside the scope of freedom of expression.

The democratic rationale for freedom of expression, and thus the legal protection of a diversity of voices, underlies the 'free exchange of opinion and availability of comprehensive information' described in the Freedom of the Press Act – that is, information 'from all sides' as the original Swedish words state. This wording illustrates how the democratic rationale involves the idea of diversity. Diverse media content, involving a wide range of subjects, information, genres and viewpoints, allows the public to participate in free and varied debate or observe others engaged in such debate (Kenyon, Svensson & Edström 2017). The state's enabling function for democratic free speech is highlighted explicitly in Sweden, where state policy has a role in promoting and deepening democracy through safeguarding free speech (SOU 1975: 79, p. 126; 1995: 37, p. 156) and to create prerequisites for plurality (Dir. 2015: 26, p. 2).

In a context like the Swedish, the conflict between the interest of an extensive right for everyone to express themselves and the interest of an environment that promote a diversity of voices (requiring measures to deal with the problem that someone silence the voices of others as may be the effect of anti-gender hate speech), is presumably balanced in another way than in a context where freedom of expression is foremost perceived as a right for everyone (in relation to state or another similar subject expected to have interest in limiting this right).

2.5.3 Limiting (restricting) or extending freedom of expression

In this section we will reflect on the various ways in which measures taken towards anti-gender hate speech might be perceived, as a limitation or an extension of freedom of expression.

Most accounts of the value of freedom of speech recognise that freedom, which we may have a right to, occasionally comes into conflict with other values (Brax 2016). A commonly held opinion is that such conflicts are solved in a way described as a restriction of freedom of expression. And absolutely, restrictions may be justified as Brax argues. Freedom of speech is not merely the absence of censorship, but there are broad senses that are of greater interest (Kenyon 2014; Karppinen 2016). Brax adds that deliberative democracy relies on voices being heard, and for free speech to realise its full potential, the conditions for participation need to be favourable. This may go way beyond the mere absence of censorship. Restrictions of free speech can therefore be justified with appeal to the values served by freedom of speech itself. There is a large set of conditions and restraints, people do not start out on an equal footing, and the conditions can hardly be described as fair. Inequality is built into this process, meaning that different agents have different capacities to begin with (Brax 2016).

Brax also points at the value of freedom as arguably based on the value of giving everyone an equal chance to succeed in his/her projects, but there is a risk that freedom combined with inequality at the outset may lead to increased inequalities. Mere procedural equality need not serve the deliberative process and may even lead to discriminatory outcomes. In this regard, equality as an ideal may easily come into conflict with freedom as an ideal. If equality is of value, this is one reason in favour of restrictions and regulations. However, such measures are particularly controversial when it comes to speech. Whereas many restrictions on speech exist, in particular in advertisement and broadcast media, any restrictions on speech are always a matter of concern (Brax 2016). Brax presents a utilitarian argument in favour of hate speech regulations with appeal to the harmful consequences of hate speech.

An alternative view to perceive a balance in favour of other values than freedom of expression is to see it as an extension of free speech rather than a restriction. It goes in line with what Brax points at, to acknowledge that freedom of expression is both non-censorship and safeguarding a diversity of voices. However, while Brax argues in favour of hate speech regulation as a justified restriction, we argue that such regulation might be understood as an extension of freedom of expression. To safeguard a diversity of voices and that no one shall be silenced might imply a code of conduct on *how* to express your opinions but not on *what* to say. No subject is banned to talk about, but the actors have to consider how they say something and to secure a space for others to give their opinions. A respectful communication does not accept hateful attacks.

To sum up, it is necessary for society to combat it by policies and regulations in order to promote democracy. If so, then how?

2.6 Legitimising the use of criminal law

Hate speech may be seen as a public wrong and do harm to individuals and groups and thus might be an issue for criminal law. As discussed above, anti-gender hate speech do not only affect individuals and groups but undermines core democratic values such as gender equality and freedom of expression, posing a significant threat to the foundations of a pluralistic and inclusive society. Addressing such societal challenges requires careful consideration of the tools available to the state, with criminal law representing the most severe and intrusive option. Its use must therefore be justified within a democratic framework, ensuring that it upholds shared values while protecting individual freedoms. It should be noted that criminal law traditionally has been a national concern, although this is changing. The justifications of criminalisation go beyond national borders even though they are valued differently.

Given the severity and intrusiveness of criminal law, its application is guided by a set of fundamental principles of criminalisation. These principles ensure that the use of criminal law is proportionate, justified, and aligned with democratic values. Keys among these are ultima ratio – the principle that criminal law should be a measure of last resort – along with the *harm principle*, the concept of public wrong, and the protection of *legal goods*. Together, these principles provide a framework for assessing when and how criminal law may legitimately be employed to address societal problems, such as anti-gender hate speech. As we shall see, these principles are essential for discussing the interplay between freedom of expression and the phenomenon of hate speech, both at the individual, group, and societal levels. In addition, these principles will be examined in relation to our theoretical perspectives, including the continuum of violence, herasure, and fragmentation.

The analysis further on will hence be anchored in present criminalisation theories and principles, as a part of contextualising and theorising the political discourse in a legal criminal setting. In Chapter 6 we will not go into detail but rather give an overview of the regulation structured out of some important criminal law principles. In this way, the discussion will be of interest outside any specific national borders. There are key guiding considerations to take into account when deciding when and what to criminalise, including the principles of harm, legal goods and public wrong. However, the influence and application of these principles vary across different legal-cultural contexts. In the Anglo-American tradition, the harm principle has been the most influential, emphasising the prevention of harm as the primary justification for criminalisation. In contrast, in the Continental, including the Scandinavian, legal systems, greater emphasis is placed on the protection of legal goods and the concept of public wrong. Here, criminalisation is often justified by the need to protect essential societal interests and maintain social order, even when it is difficult to demonstrate individual harm (Peršak 2006; Puig 2008). It should be noted that the continental criminal legal systems have not focused on the grounds for criminalisation, even though there are fundamental principles, such as the principles regulating criminalisation and implementation: ultima ratio; the *principle of conformity*; the *principle of guilt*; the *principle of legality*; the principle of proportionality; and the *principle of humanity*. As the continental systems are built on political decisions rather than case law, the legal theories have a less influence in the continental systems, including the Scandinavian legal systems. Nevertheless, or perhaps precisely because of this, the ideas and motivations underlying criminalisation require careful scrutiny and reflection, particularly in an era of populist criminal justice policymaking.

Mill famously articulated the harm principle in his 1859 essay 'On Liberty', asserting. The only purpose for which power can be rightfully exercised over any member of a civilised community, against his will, is to prevent harm to others.' For Mill, the harm principle represents the sole legitimate ground for criminalisation, understood as a negative constraint: where there is no harm, there should be no criminalisation (Mill 1859). Feinberg, a more contemporary 20th-century theorist, however, adopts a broader approach. While he acknowledges the harm principle as an important justification for criminalisation, he does not view it as the only legitimate ground. Feinberg frames the harm principle in a more positive sense, as an active reason to support criminalisation in the presence of harm. In addition, Feinberg introduces the *offence principle*, which holds that the prevention of serious offence to others can also justify criminalisation, expanding the scope beyond just the harm principle. Feinberg also makes a distinction between private and public harm, to go beyond the individual. However, he underlines that the public consists of individuals, and that the term public interest is vague, and application may be hard to make (Feinberg 1984). The harm principle may be well-suited for criminalising anti-gender hate speech directed at individuals, especially the more severe forms, such as those categorised as hate speech in a narrow sense discussed above. However, for this principle to adequately capture the gravity of anti-gender hate speech, harm must be understood in a contextualised manner, consistent with the continuum of violence. This approach recognises individual actions as both part of and legitimising a continuum that escalates into more severe forms of harm. Furthermore, following Feinberg's broader conception of harm, the principle can also support the criminalising of anti-gender hate speech at the group and potentially societal levels. Feinberg's framework extends the notion of harm beyond the individual. A narrow interpretation of actions, aligned with Mill's understanding of harm, risks minimising the problem and may align with the societal tendency towards herasure (Manne 2018).

In German legal doctrine ideas and theories on the Rechtsgüter have been crucial in the discussion on legitimacy and limits of criminal law (Jareborg 2005). This can be translated into legal goods, legally protected interests of individuals or other entities or certain collectives. This may include natural material (land and water) and products of human activities (food, money et cetera) and immaterial goods (privacy, education, freedom and security; Peršak 2006). Duff (2018) defines it as 'a good which the law properly recognises as being necessary for social peace or for individual wellbeing, and as therefore meriting legal protection'. This principle is well-suited to addressing anti-gender hate speech at the individual, group, and potentially societal levels. It may align with the category of immaterial goods proposed by Peršak (2006), encompassing goods recognised by society as essential for social peace (at the group and societal levels) and for individual well-being (at the individual and group levels), as suggested by Duff.

Public wrong can be used to capture an offence committed against a community. The state will be a party in the proceedings against public wrong. In a Swedish legal context, the offence agitation against a population group, which constitutes an example of what is covered by the concept hate speech, is defined within the group of offences that target the state and public interest. The principle of public wrong clearly justifies the criminalisation of anti-gender hate speech at the societal level, encompassing both group and societal dimensions.

When Jareborg discusses the fundamental principles of criminal law, he does not arrange them in any specific order, but often the *principle of ultima ratio* is mentioned first as it regulates when an act should be criminalised. The principle states that criminalisation should be the last resort to handle societal problems. It is, according to Jareborg, a 'principle of legislative ethics'. As societal problems could and should be met by various/different means provided by the state (education, taxes ... or criminalisation) there has to be a proper reflection and justification to use criminalisation as the means. As criminalisation means that the state causes an individual pain intentionally, it infringes the ethical principle not to cause others harm.

The principle is sometimes used to justify the fragmentary character of criminal law, as criminal law is only used to protect some legal goods and also the subsidiary character of criminal law (Jareborg 2005). Jareborg also argues that the principle of ultima ratio can be recognised as an overarching, meta principle. Peršak argues that the principle should not only be perceived as a legal principle prior to criminalisation, but as relevant to law in general and prior to any state intervention. And the principle speaks, she argues, not only to the lawmaker but to any official or body within the criminal legal system (Peršak 2006, 123). However, the principle of ultima ratio speaks primarily to the law maker and will hence be discussed in this book only in relation to the legislation process and criminal legal system as such. Peršak also connects the principle to the presumption of *in dubio pro libertate*, meaning when in doubt, do not criminalise, that is, the law maker should not use criminalisation to deal with a specific problem unless there is evidence that the criminalisation is necessary (Peršak 2006; see also Feinberg 1984, 9).

A second principle is *the principle of conformity* (in Swedish criminal legal theory) stating that a punishment may only be used when the person that risks a punishment has the ability and possibility to obey the law. This is closely linked to the principle of guilt, and the principle of legality. The *principle of guilt* means that only a person that demonstrated guilt should be subject to criminal punishment. An accident is not ground for criminal liability.

Principle of legality is sometimes described as one of the most crucial ones. It holds that no one should be imposed criminal liability without a legal foundation. The core of it is a demand on the normative nature (*normbundendhet*) of the exercise of power as opposed to arbitrariness.

The principle of legality is enshrined in the Swedish Constitution, *Regeringsformen* (RF – The instrument of government) stating that public authority is exercised under the law (chapter 1, section 1). This principle applies to all governmental actions, ensuring that power is exercised according to established legal norms rather than arbitrary decisions. It is a cornerstone for safeguarding individual legal security by promoting predictability in legal processes.

In the context of criminal law, the principle of legality is particularly stringent due to its implications for individual freedoms. This principle mandates restrictive interpretation of criminal statutes and prohibits analogical application of the law. As stipulated in RF chapter 2, section 10, no one can be punished for an act that was not subject to criminal penalties when committed, nor can a more severe penalty be imposed retroactively.

The principle of legality comprises four sub-principles:

The prohibition of judgment without statutory basis (*praeter legem* prohibition).

The prohibition of retroactivity, ensuring that laws not in effect at the time of the crime cannot be applied.

The prohibition of analogy, which forbids extending the application of laws beyond their literal meaning.

The prohibition against vague or unclear laws, which requires that legal provisions, particularly criminal statutes, must be sufficiently clear to allow individuals to foresee the consequences of their actions. This criterion is typically assessed from a legal expert's perspective.

In most instances, these principles do not pose practical challenges. However, the prohibition against vague laws may encounter difficulties, particularly when dealing with references to EU regulations or inconsistencies in legislative amendments (Asp, Ulväng & Jareborg 2013).

The principle of proportionality is fundamental in ensuring that the severity of punishments reflects the gravity of the offence. Society's view of particular crimes is mirrored in the applicable sentencing ranges, with offences against life and health typically receiving harsher penalties than crimes against property. The proportionality principle dictates that punishments must be commensurate with the harm caused by the criminal act. Moreover, this principle must be observed during sentencing in individual cases, ensuring that the severity of the punishment corresponds to the seriousness of the crime (Asp, Ulväng & Jareborg 2013).

Closely related is the *principle of humanity*, which holds that, in a civilised society, the state should not impose unnecessary suffering on those who have committed crimes. This principle acts as a safeguard against excessive or inhumane punishment, reinforcing the notion that justice must be tempered with mercy (Asp, Ulväng & Jareborg 2013).

The doctrine of legal goods and the principle of ultima ratio stresses that criminal law should only be used as the last resort. The starting point is then that criminal law is an evil and should only be employed when it is entirely necessary, and the doctrine of legal goods and public wrong might function as a guidance to answer the question of when it is necessary to use criminalisation. The balance between the legal goods that need protection and the use of criminalisation as a last resort underlines the importance of looking at the problem of anti-gender hate speech from a structural perspective and going beyond the individuals involved. It is also of importance to take into account that as the criminal legal system contains and upholds structural discrimination the use of criminalisation should be utterly restrictive (Burman 2010; Bumiller 2009).

Having said that, a compelling reason to consider criminal law as a tool to combat anti-gender hate speech is, firstly, that research highlights gaps in the criminal legal system which, in practice, result in weak and fragmented legal protection for women. This, in turn, poses a barrier to ensuring women's freedom of movement in digital spaces and securing their voices in public discourse. Secondly, criminal law carries significant symbolic value and is, therefore, essential in shaping and changing societal norms.

To be able to discuss criminalisation, and the relation to gender equality and freedom of expression, we also need to readdress the question of what anti-gender hate speech really is, and hence, what kinds of actions that should fall within and outside the criminal legal sphere.

In sum, the harm principle posits that criminal law should intervene when actions cause harm to others. It should be noted that the harm principle is primary in the Anglo-American systems (Peršak 2006). The legal goods principle is more prevalent in the continental legal tradition and focuses on the protection of crucial societal interests, such as life, health, and property, justifying criminalisation when these are at risk (Asp, Ulväng & Jareborg 2013). Finally, the concept of public wrong holds that actions may be criminalised when they violate societal norms or values, thus constituting a wrong against the community at large. These principles collectively ensure that the criminalisation process is both justifiable and measured, balancing societal protection with individual rights (Peršak 2006).

In the Nordic countries, however, the harm principle is less central to the justification for criminalisation. Legislation may be enacted even when it is difficult to prove intent to cause harm, as the focus shifts to the effect of the act rather than the intent behind it.

2.7 Concluding remarks

This chapter has presented the theoretical perspectives and democratic framework that underpin our analysis of anti-gender hate speech. Central to this approach is the *Nordic gaze*, which combines the region's commitment to gender equality and democracy with feminist theoretical tools. This lens enables us to critically examine anti-gender hate speech as a systemic problem that transcends individual harm, affecting societal structures and democratic principles.

Anti-gender hate speech is conceptualised in this book through three interrelated dimensions. First, it is seen as an obstacle to gender equality, given its roots in gender stereotypes and its manifestation as gender-based violence. Second, it is understood as a restriction on freedom of expression when the concept is defined broadly to encompass not only non-censorship but also the active promotion of a diversity of voices. Third, it is analysed through the lens of criminalisation principles – such as the harm principle, the common good and *public wrong*. These principles provide a framework for critically assessing how and when criminal law can be employed as a tool to address online anti-gender hate speech, balancing the need for regulation with the democratic imperative to protect freedom of expression.

This chapter has outlined the theoretical tools that will guide the analysis in the following chapters. Concepts such as Kelly's continuum of violence, Manne's himpathy and herasure, and the interplay between freedom of expression and gender equality will be used to frame and interpret the regulatory frameworks under review. By framing anti-gender hate speech within a broader democratic context, we underscore its far-reaching consequences – not just for individuals but for the public sphere and societal structures at large.

In Chapters 3–6, we provide an overview of current regulations addressing hate speech within the fields of gender equality, freedom of expression, and criminal law. This overview sets the stage for analysing how anti-gender hate speech is addressed – or overlooked – across different jurisdictions. In Chapter 7, we revisit these theoretical frameworks in light of empirical findings, using them to propose normative solutions for addressing anti-gender hate speech as a democratic challenge.

Notes

1 Men who lives in involuntary celibacy.

2 Regeringskansliet 2016. Jämställdhetsmålen: publ. 21 dec. www.regeringen.se/regeringens-politik/jamstalldhet/mal-for-jamstalldhet/ (accessed 2024-09-15).

3 Freedom of information refers to the constitutionally protected *Right of access to information held by public authorities*: 'Principen att de handlingar som förvaras hos statliga och kommunala myndigheter är allmänt tillgängliga är ett karakteristiskt inslag i den offentliga rätten i vårt land. De grundläggande bestämmelserna i ämnet återfinns i grundlag, ... 1949 års tryckfrihetsförordning, medan föreskrifter som innebär begränsningar i principen är intagna främst i en särskild lag, ... nämligen sekretesslagen.' ['The principle that documents held by state and municipal authorities are publicly accessible is a characteristic feature of public law in our country. The fundamental provisions on this subject are found in the constitution, ... the 1949 Freedom of the Press Act, while provisions imposing limitations on this principle are primarily contained in a specific law, ... namely the Secrecy Act."] (prop. 1975/76: 160, 14).

References

Literature

Alexy, R. & Rivers, J. (2010), *A theory of constitutional rights*. Oxford University Press.

Andersson, U. (2004), *Hans (ord) eller hennes? en könsteoretisk analys av straffrättsligt skydd mot sexuella övergrepp*. Bokbox.

Andersson, U. (2011), 'Våld mot kvinnor och straffrätt'. In Svensson, E.-M., Andersson, U., Brækhus, H. Burman, M., Hellum, A., Jørgensen, S. & Pylkkänen, A. (Eds.), *På vei: kjønn og rett i Norden*. Makadam.

Asp, P., Ulväng, M. & Jareborg, N. (2013), *Kriminalrättens grunder*. Iustus förlag.
Barker, K. & Jurasz, O. (2020), 'Online violence against women as an obstacle to gender equality: A critical view from Europe', *European Equality Law Review*, 1, 47–60.
Bladini, M. (2013), *I objektivitetens sken: en kritisk granskning av objektivitetsideal, objektivitetsanspråk och legitimeringsstrategier i diskurser om dömande i brottmål.* Makadam.
Bladini, M. (2020), 'Silenced voices. Online violence targeting women as a threat to democracy', *Nordic Journal on Law and Society*, 3(2), 1–42.
Bladini, M. & Svedberg Andersson, W. (2020), 'Swedish rape legislation from use of force to voluntariness: Critical reflections from an everyday life perspective', *Bergen Journal of Criminal Law and Criminal Justice*, 8(2), 95–125. https://doi.org/10.15845/bjclcj.v8i2.3241.
Bollinger, L. C. (1986), *The tolerant society*. Oxford University Press.
Brax, D. (2016), 'Hate speech and the distribution of the costs and benefits of freedom of speech'. In Edström, M., Kenyon, A. T. & Svensson, E-M. (Eds.), *Blurring the lines: Market-driven and democracy-driven freedom of expression*. Nordicom.
Bumiller, K. (2009), *In an abusive state: How neoliberalism appropriated the feminist movement against sexual assault*. Duke University Press.
Burman, M. (2007), *Straffrätt och mäns våld mot kvinnor: om straffrättens förmåga att producera jämställdhet*. Iustus.
Burman, M. (2010), 'The ability of criminal law to produce gender equality: Judicial discourses in the Swedish criminal legal system', *Violence against Women*, 16(2), 173–188. https://doi.org/10.1177/1077801209355515.
Carlsson, A. (2024), *Constitutional protection of freedom of expression in the age of social media: A comparative study*. Department of Law, Uppsala University.
Carlsson, U. (Ed.) (2016), 'Freedom of expression and media in transition: Studies and reflections in the digital age', *Nordicom Review*. Göteborg: Nordicom.
Conaghan, J. (2013), *Law and gender*, 1st ed. Oxford University Press. https://doi.org/10.1093/acprof:oso/9780199592920.001.0001.
Cook, R. J. & Cusack, S. (2010), *Gender stereotyping transnational legal perspectives*. University of Pennsylvania Press.
Duff, A. (2018), 'Theories of criminal law'. In Zalta, E. N. & Nodelman, U. (Eds.), *Stanford encyclopedia of philosophy*. https://plato.stanford.edu/entries/criminal-law/ (accessed 2024-11-28).
Edström, M. & Svensson, E.-M. (2016), 'Trust and values for sale. Market-driven and democracy-driven freedom of expression'. In Carlsson, U. (Ed.), *Freedom of expression and media in transition. Studies and reflections in the digital age*. Nordicom.
Feinberg, J. (1984), *Harm to others: The moral limits of the criminal law*. Oxford University Press.
Fejős, A. & Zenta, V. (Eds.) (2021), *Anti-gender hate speech in populist right-wing social media communication*. http://genha.eu/sites/default/files/pdf/Anti-Gender%20Hate%20Speech%20in%20Populist%20Right-Wing%20Social%20Media%20Communication_0.pdf.
Franzén, A. & Gottzén, L. (2020), *Våldsprevention i Sverige: En forskningsöversikt*. Barn- och ungdomsvetenskap.
Fredman, S. (2022), Discrimination law, 3rd ed. Oxford University Press. https://doi.org/10.1093/oso/9780198854081.001.0001.

Gunnarsson, Å., Svensson, E.-M. & Davies, M. (2007), *Exploiting the limits of law: Swedish feminism and the challenge to pessimism*. Ashgate.

Gustafsson, H. & Svensson, E-M. (2024), 'Is the rights-based approach to social justice (really) the right way? Rightification and the question of social injustice', *Nordic Journal on Law and Society*, 7(2), 1–28.

Hellum, A. & Aasen, H. S. (2013), *Women's human rights: CEDAW in international, regional and national law*. Cambridge University Press.

Hellum, A., Ikdahl, I., Blaker Strand, V. & Svensson, E.-M. (2024), *Nordic equality and anti-discrimination laws in the throes of change: Legal developments in Sweden, Finland, Norway, and Iceland*. Taylor & Francis. https://doi.org/10.4324/9781003172840.

Holtmaat, H. M. T. (2013), 'CEDAW: A holistic approach to women's equality and freedom'. In Hellum, A. & Sinding-Aasen H. S. (Eds.), *Women's human rights: CEDAW in international, regional and national law*. Cambridge University Press.

Jareborg, N. (2005), 'Criminalization as last resort (ultima ratio)', *Ohio State Journal of Criminal Law*, 2(2), 521–534.

Karppinen, K. (2016), 'Beyond positive and negative conceptions of free speech'. In Edström, M., Kenyon, A. T. & Svensson, E.-M. (Eds.), *Blurring the lines: Market-driven and democracy-driven freedom of expression*. Nordicom.

Kelly, L. (1988), *Surviving sexual violence*. John Wiley and Sons.

Kenyon, A. T. (2014), 'Assuming free speech', *Modern Law Review*, 77(3), 379–408. https://doi.org/10.1111/1468-2230.12071.

Kenyon, A. T. (2016), 'Who, what, why and how. Questions for positive free speech and media systems'. In Edström, M., Kenyon, A. T. & Svensson, E.-M. (Eds.), *Blurring the lines: Market-driven and democracy-driven freedom of expression*. Nordicom.

Kenyon, A. T. (2021), *Democracy of expression: Positive free speech and law*. Cambridge University Press.

Kenyon, A. T., Svensson, E.-M. & Edström, M. (2017), 'Building and sustaining freedom of expression: Considering Sweden', *Nordicom Review*, 38(1), 31–45. https://doi.org/10.1515/nor-2016-0043.

Lagiewska, M. (2024), 'Online hate speech under international law'. In Wagner, A. & Marusek, S. (Eds.), *Handbook on cyber hate: The modern cyber evil*. Springer.

Lichtenberg, J. (1990), 'Foundations and limits of freedom of the press'. In Lichtenberg, J. (Ed.), *Democracy and the mass media: A collection of essays*. Cambridge University Press.

Lührmann, A., Tannenberg, M. & Lindberg, S. I. (2018), 'Regimes of the world (RoW): Opening new avenues for the comparative study of political regimes', *Politics and Governance*, 6(1), 60–77. https://doi.org/10.17645/pag.v6i1.1214.

Lundgren, E., Heimer, G., Westerstrand, J. & Kalliokoski, A.-M. (2002), *Captured queen men's violence against women in 'equal' Sweden: A prevalence study*. Brottsoffermyndigheten.

MacKinnon, C. A. (2016), 'Rape redefined', *Harvard Law & Policy Review*, 10(2), 431–477.

Malleson, K. (2003), 'Justifiying gender equality on the bench: Why difference wont' do', *Feminist Legal Studies*, 11, 1–24.

Manne, K. (2018), *Down girl: The logic of misogyny*. Oxford University Press.

McGlynn, C., Rackley, E. & Houghton, R. (2017), 'Beyond "revenge porn": The continuum of image-based sexual abuse', *Feminist Legal Studies*, 25(1), 25–46.

Mill, J. S. (1991, orig. 1859), *On liberty and other essays.* Oxford University Press.

Naffine, N. (2002), 'Can women be legal persons?' In *Visible women: Essays on feminist legal theory and political philosophy.* Hart.

Peršak, N. (2006), *Criminalising harmful conduct. The harm principle, its limits and continental Counterparts.* Springer.

Petäjä, U. (2006), *Varför yttrandefrihet? om rättfärdigandet av yttrandefrihet med utgångspunkt från fem centrala argument i den demokratiska idétraditionen.* Växjö University Press.

Puig, S. M. (2008), 'Legal goods protected by the law and legal goods protected by the criminal law as limits to the state's power to criminalize conduct', *New Criminal Law Review*, 11(3), 409–418. https://doi.org/10.1525/nclr.2008.11.3.409.

Pylkkänen, A. (2009), *Trapped in equality: Women as legal persons in the modernisation of Finnish law.* Suomalaisen Kirjallisuuden Seura.

Roy, A. (1997), *The god of small things.* Harper Collins.

Smart, C. (2002), *Feminism and the power of law.* Taylor & Francis.

Smith, D. E. (2012), *Everyday world as problematic: A feminist sociology*, 1st ed. Northeastern University Press.

Svedberg, W. (2013), *Ett (o)jämställt transportsystem i gränslandet mellan politik och rätt – En genusrättsvetenskaplig studie av rättslig styrning för jämställdhet inom vissa samhällsområden.* Bokbox förlag.

Svensson, E.-M. (1997), *Genus och rätt en problematisering av föreställningen om rätten.* Iustus.

Svensson, E.-M. (2016), 'Upholding the division between editorial and commercial content in legislation and self-regulation'. In *Blurring the lines: Market-driven and democracy-driven freedom of expression.* Nordicom.

Svensson, E.-M. (2020), 'Exploiting justice in a transformative Swedish society', *Nordic Journal on Law and Society*, 3(2), 1–25.

Svensson, E.-M. (2021), 'Law and governance'. In *Pan-Arctic report.* Gender Equality in the Arctic.

Svensson, E.-M. (2025), 'Gender equality'. In Graham, B. & Krunke, H. (Eds.), *Nordic cooperation and the European Union: 50 years of legal integration.* Hart.

Svensson, E.-M. & Edström, M. (2014), 'Freedom of expression vs. gender equality: Conflicting values when regulating gender stereotypes in advertising', *Tidsskrift for Rettsvitenskap*, 127(5), 479–511.

Svensson, E.-M. & Edström, M. (2016), 'Market-driven challenges to freedom of expression and the interaction between the state, the market, and the media', *Nordicom Review*, 37(2), 1–16. https://doi.org/10.1515/nor-2016-0013.

Svensson, E.-M. & Gunnarsson, Å. (2012), 'Gender equality in the welfare state', *feminists@law*, 2(1), 1–27.

Syvertsen, T., Enli, G., Mjøs, O. J. & Moe, H. (2014), *The media welfare state: Nordic media in the digital era.* The University of Michigan Press.

Uhnoo, S., Wettergren, Å. & Bladini, M. (2024), 'It could have been my son! Himpathy and the male fear defence in rape trials', *Journal of Law and Society*, 51(4), 562–585.

Wettergren, Å., Uhnoo, S. & Bladini, M. (2025), *Challenging legal core values: Consent-based rape legislation in practice*, Bristol University Press.

Public documents and laws

International (UN)

Convention on the Elimination of All Forms of Discrimination against Women (CEDAW), New York, 18 Dec. 1979, entered into force 3 Sep. 1981. www.ohchr.org/sites/default/files/cedaw.pdf (accessed 2024-10-23).

General Recommendation no. 25, on article 4, paragraph 1, of the Convention on the Elimination of All Forms of Discrimination against Women, on temporary special measures. www.un.org/womenwatch/daw/cedaw/recommendations/General%20recommendation%2025%20(English).pdf (accessed 2024-11-19).

General Recommendation no. 35, on gender-based violence against women, updating General Recommendation no. 19. www.right-to-education.org/sites/right-to-education.org/files/resource-attachments/CEDAW_C_GC_35_8267_E.pdf (accessed 2024-11-19).

International Convention on the Elimination of All Forms of Racial Discrimination (ICERD), New York, 21 Dec. 1965, entered into force 4 Jan. 1969. www.ohchr.org/en/instruments-mechanisms/instruments/international-convention-elimination-all-forms-racial (accessed 2024-12-01).

United Nations (n.d.a), 'Gender equality'. ww.un.org/en/global-issues/gender-equality (accessed 2024-11-19).

United Nations (n.d.b), 'What is hate speech?' www.un.org/en/hate-speech/understanding-hate-speech/what-is-hate-speech (accessed 2024-11-19).

Universal Declaration of Human Rights (UDHR) (10 Dec. 1948), U.N.G.A. Res. 217 A (III) (1948). www.ohchr.org/en/human-rights/universal-declaration/translations/english (accessed 2024-10-23).

International (Council of Europe and EU)

European Convention on Human Rights (ECHR). www.echr.coe.int/documents/convention_eng.pdf (accessed 2024-10-23).

European Institute for Gender Equality (EIGE) as amended by Protocols Nos. 11, 14 and 15 supplemented by Protocols Nos. 1, 4, 6, 7, 12, 13 and 16 (2024). https://eige.europa.eu/publications-resources/thesaurus/terms/1059?language_content_entity=en (accessed 2024-10-23).

Sweden

Dir. 2015: 26, *En mediepolitik för framtiden*. Kulturdepartementet. www.regeringen.se/contentassets/37c5138b3218403f8c31bbf1658c4e48/en-mediepolitik-for-framtiden-dir.-201526 (accessed 2024-10-24).

Gender Equality Policy in Sweden (2024). www.government.se/information-material/2019/03/gender-equality-policy-in-sweden/ (accessed 2024-08-30).

Prop. 1997/98: 55. *Kvinnofrid*. www.regeringen.se/contentassets/1733625e719c43b28f073fa9cdec90f2/kvinnofrid-prop.-19979855 (accessed 2024-11-27).

Regeringskansliet 2016. Jämställdhetsmålen: publ. 21 dec. www.regeringen.se/regeringens-politik/jamstalldhet/mal-for-jamstalldhet/. (accessed 2024-09-15)

SOU 1975: 79, *Svensk Press. Statlig presspolitik* Betänkande av 1972 års pressutredning. Göteborgs Offsettryckeri AB. https://filedn.com/ljdBas5OJsrLJOq6KhtBYC4/forarbeten/sou/1975/sou-1975-79.pdf (accessed 2024-11-27).

SOU 1990: 44, *Demokrati och makt i Sverige*. Maktutredningens huvudrapport. https://lagen.nu/sou/1990:44?attachment=index.pdf&repo=soukb&dir=downloaded (accessed 2024-11-27).
SOU 1995: 37, *Vårt dagliga blad – stöd till svensk dagspress*. Betänkande av Pressutredningen -94. Fritzes, Offentliga Publikationer. https://lagen.nu/sou/1995:37?attachment=index.pdf&repo=soukb&dir=downloaded (accessed 2024-11-27).
SOU 2000: 1, *En uthållig demokrati! – Politik för folkstyrelse på 2000-talet*. Slutbetänkande från Demokratiutredningen. Fritzes Offentliga Publikationer. www.regeringen.se/contentassets/69008696fa114a81837274bbf623793b/en-uthallig-demokrati---politik-for-folkstyrelse-pa-2000-talet/ (accessed 2024-11-27).
SOU 2016: 5, *Låt fler forma framtiden!* Betänkande av 2014 års Demokratiutredning–Delaktighet och jämlikt inflytande. Wolters Kluwer Sverige AB. www.regeringen.se/rattsliga-dokument/statens-offentliga-utredningar/2016/01/sou-20165/ (accessed 2024-11-27).
SOU 2022: 28, *Vår demokrati – värd att värna varje dag*. Betänkande av kommittén Demokratin 100 år – samling för en stark demokrati. Elanders Sverige AB, Stockholm 2022. www.regeringen.se/rattsliga-dokument/statens-offentliga-utredningar/2022/06/sou-202228/ (accessed 2024-11-27).
Vad är demokrati? (2023). www.riksdagen.se/sv/sa-fungerar-riksdagen/demokrati/vad-ar-demokrati/ (accessed 2024-10-24).

Other sources

Economist Intelligence Unit (2006–2023). 'Our world in data'. https://ourworldindata.org/grapher/democracy-index-eiu (accessed 2024-10-24).
Varieties of Democracy (V-Dem). www.v-dem.net/ (accessed 2024-10-24).

3 Visiting the sphere of regulation

In the following chapters 4–6 we will present an overview of the most important regulation in the areas of gender equality, freedom of expression and criminal law on UN, European, EU and national level.[1] The legal instruments and policies adopted by the Council of Europe and EU oblige the States to follow them, and thus they are applicable in the States together with the national legislation. For instance, EU Directives must be implemented in national legal orders directly or indirectly. They have also a more general impact on the national level. The Member States have moreover influence on the Council of Europe and EU. The driving forces for measures to deal with anti-gender hate speech may therefore come from both upwards and downwards. For instance, the Nordic countries have previously been influential when it comes to the field of gender equality (Svensson 2025). The overview in these chapters will nuance this picture.

The regulation at a UN level hence includes declarations, conventions, comments by the monitoring bodies and other UN bodies as well as policies, recommendations etc. The conventions are legally binding for ratifying State parties. Other instruments might, if not legally binding, still be morally or politically binding.

The regulation at a European level includes legislation (treaties, conventions, constitutional acts, regulations, directives, decisions, etc.) and policies, recommendations, guidelines and good practices etc. The legal instruments are binding for the member states of the Council of Europe and in the EU, respectively.[2] The EU is based on the rule of law, and there are two main types of EU law – primary and secondary. Primary law is at the top of the hierarchy of norms and consist of EU's constituent treaties; the Charter of Fundamental rights; and the general principles established by the Court of Justice of the EU. Secondary law comprises both legislative and non-legislative acts adopted by the EU institutions (European Union 2023). The concepts crucial in EU gender equality policy are shaped by rulings from the European Court of Justice. Documents from the special commissions of the Council of Europe – the European Parliament, the European Commission, Council of the European Union, Committee of Ministers and the Parliamentary Assembly – may not be legally binding, but they are important instruments for how to

DOI: 10.4324/9781003383062-3

interpret and apply the relevant legal sources (European Commission n.d.). The European Parliament's standing committee, the Committee on Women's Rights and Gender Equality, has also an important function when it comes to anti-gender hate speech. Regulation and policies at the EU level can be described as fragmented due to the division into several legislative and policymaking bodies and to the challenges to find and thus access the legal and policy instruments.

The regulation at the national level includes legislation (constitutional acts, statutes) and policies such as action plans etc. The national level is exemplified with Sweden, Italy and Spain, all Member States of Council of Europe and EU.

Notes

1 For a more comprehensive presentation we refer to the *Report on the state of the art on anti-gender hate speech* (Antigona Research Group 2020). The presentation of gender equality and non-discrimination below is in addition also based on the chapter 'Law and governance' in the *Pan-Arctic report on gender equality* (Svensson 2021).

2 They are also in general binding for the European Economic Area (EEA).

References

Literature

Antigona Research Group (2020), *Report on the state of the art on anti-gender hate speech*. https://cris.unibo.it/retrieve/e1dcb335-f518-7715-e053-1705fe0a6cc9/REPORT%20ON%20THE%20STATE%20OF%20THE%20ART%20ON%20ANTI%20GENDER%20HATE%20SPEECH.pdf.

Svensson, E.-M. (2021), 'Law and governance'. In *Pan-Arctic report*. Gender Equality in the Arctic.

Svensson, E-M. (2025), 'Gender equality'. In Graham, B. & Krunke, H. (Eds.), *Nordic cooperation and the European Union: 50 years of legal integration*. Hart.

Public documents and laws

International (Council of Europe and EU)

European Commission (n.d.), 'Types of EU law', https://commission.europa.eu/law/law-making-process/types-eu-law_en (accessed 2024-11-20).

European Union (2023), 'EU hierarchy of norms', https://eur-lex.europa.eu/EN/legal-content/glossary/eu-hierarchy-of-norms.html (accessed 2024-11-20).

4 Anti-gender hate speech counteracts gender equality

We apply a comprehensive approach to anti-gender hate speech that it is counteracting gender equality and may constitute discrimination against women, as both *gender stereotypes* and *violence against women*, a starting point that is in compliance with an increasing body of policies and legislation. This position has been increasingly claimed and strengthened over the years on a global level and international commitments to target anti-gender hate speech to promote and achieve gender equality have been intensified. As the UN Special Rapporteur Irene Khan has declared, 'When women raise their voices, too often they are suppressed. In the digital age, the Internet has become the new battleground in the struggle for women's rights, amplifying opportunities for women to express themselves but also multiplying possibilities for repression' (A/76/258, 2021). The pressure on States, as parties to legal and political instruments and as members of inter-governmental agreements, to take action against anti-gender hate speech has as a consequence increased. The expectations progressively take the form of obligations, legally and politically. In addition, the expectations and obligations for other actors than the States, such as for example social media platforms, are also strengthened. However, we focus on the obligations and expectations on the public bodies here.

4.1 Gender equality

Gender equality is a goal for the global society, widely declared in legal instruments, in political agendas and agreements. According to the foundation of the body of human rights law, the Universal Declaration of Human Rights (UDHR) adopted in 1948, all human beings are born equal in dignity and rights (Art. 1). Most States support the fundamental principles set forth in the UDHR, a common standard of achievements for all peoples and all nations. Along with the UDHR the International Covenant on Civil and Political Rights (ICCPR) and the International Covenant on Economic, Social and Cultural Rights (ICESCR), both of which entered into force

DOI: 10.4324/9781003383062-4

1976, form the 'international bill of rights'. These two treaties reflect the principles of the UDHR in binding form. Most States are parties to ICCPR and to ICESCR. ICCPR and ICESCR are monitored by the Human Rights Committee and Committee on Economic, Social and Cultural Rights, respectively (Svensson 2021).

The principle of equal rights of men and women is declared in the mentioned treaties. For example, the ICCPR states:

> Art. 3 The States Parties to the present Covenant undertake to ensure the equal right of men and women to the enjoyment of all civil and political rights set forth in the present Covenant.

Women's human rights are targeted in specific in The Convention on the Elimination of All Forms of Discrimination against Women (CEDAW). The spirit of this important UN legal instrument to ensure women's human rights is rooted in the goals of the United Nations: to reaffirm faith in fundamental human rights, in the dignity, and worth of the human person, in the equal rights of men and women. According to the Special Rapporteur on violence against women the core international human rights instruments, including those on women's rights, are to be interpreted in a transformative way. Thus, even if they were drafted before the advent of information and communications technology (ICT), the human rights instruments obviously provide a global and dynamic set of rights and obligations with transformative potential and they could play a key role in the promotion and protection of fundamental human rights, including a woman's rights to live a life free from violence, including anti-gender hate speech (A/HRC/38/47).

The most important worldwide acknowledged action plan is the 2030 Agenda for Sustainable Development and the SDGs (Transforming Our World 2015). While the concept of gender equality is not directly defined, there is an assumption of its correlation to power. Gender equality can be understood as specific to women as well as to the relationship between men and women, often understood in terms of shared power and responsibility. This perception is, since the beginning of the 1990s, explicitly declared in the Swedish government's gender equality policy, in the wordings 'women and men shall have the same power to shape society and their own lives' (Gender Equality Policy in Sweden 2024).

In the preamble of the Protocol No. 12 to the Convention for the Protection of Human Rights and Fundamental Freedoms, the Member States of the Council of Europe declare that all persons are equal before the law and are entitled to the equal protection of the law. And, in the Council of Europe's Gender Equality Strategy (2024–2029; CM(2024)17-final), it is stated: 'We recall that gender equality and the full, equal and effective participation of women in public and private decision-making processes are essential to the rule of law, democracy and sustainable development. We underline the pioneering role of the Council of Europe, including through the Istanbul Convention, in the fight against violence against women and domestic violence.'

Equality between women and men is one of the key objectives of the European Union, enshrined in the European Treaties, particularly in Articles 2 and 3(3) of the Treaty on European Union (TEU), Articles 8, 10, 19, 153 and 157 of the Treaty on the Functioning of the European Union (TFEU) and Articles 21 and 23 of the Charter of Fundamental Rights. The European Parliament expresses high ambitions concerning the promotion of gender equality (European Parliament 2024).

4.2 Means to achieve gender equality: Non-discrimination and gender mainstreaming

The means to achieve gender equality are, as indicated above, depending on the perception of it and on the context. In legal texts the formal interpretation initially correlated to the non-discrimination principle. This principle is expressed in many important legal instruments. How a gender-equal situation looks and which path leads to gender equality may vary, and it might be easier to identify what is not gender equality. Often, gender equality or equal rights of men and women are perceived as absence of discrimination on the basis of sex/gender, in specific in legal contexts (Svensson 2021). *Equal rights of men and women* and *non-discrimination* are thus corresponding legal concepts to gender equality (see, e.g., ICCPR Arts. 3 and 26; CEDAW Art. 1).

The human rights instruments promise non-discrimination, and ICCPR and International Covenant on Economic, Social and Cultural Rights (ICESCR) also have a self-standing provision that promises equal enjoyment of the human rights in the treaties.

The European Convention for the Protection of Human Rights and Fundamental Freedoms (ECHR) also contains a prohibition of discrimination in Art. 14. The enjoyment of the rights and freedoms set forth in the Convention shall be secured without discrimination on any ground such as, among several characteristics, sex.

The non-discrimination principle is declared also in Articles 2 and 3(3) TEU and Article 10 in TFEU.

Another mean to promote gender equality is the gender mainstreaming strategy, established in the 1990s, for example in Sweden in 1994 (Svensson & Gunnarsson 2012), and globally a year after. In addition to the legal principles of equal rights of men and women and non-discrimination a strategy for promoting gender equality was established in the key global policy document on gender equality Beijing Platform for Action in 1995: *gender mainstreaming*. Most definitions of gender mainstreaming conform to the UN Economic and Social Council's (ECOSOC) formally defined concept: 'Mainstreaming a gender perspective is the process of assessing the implications for women and men of any planned action, including legislation, policies, or programmes in all areas and at all levels' (ECOSOC 1997). The platform is a strategy for making women's as well as men's concerns and experiences an integral dimension of the design, implementation, monitoring and evaluation of policies and programmes in all political, economic, and societal spheres so that women and men benefit equally, and inequality is not perpetuated. The goal is to achieve gender equality. The strategy may serve as a pushy force if used in the intended way. The platform is monitored by the principal global intergovernmental body CSW (Commission on the Status of Women), exclusively dedicated to the promotion of gender equality, the rights and the empowerment of women. CSW is a functional commission of ECOSOC, established already in 1946.

Gender mainstreaming is since the 1990s increasingly a policy tool that is widely used by national governments and international organisations. The gender mainstreaming strategy has been an integral part of the work and activities of the Council of Europe to promote the full realisation of gender equality since the 1990s (Council of Europe [CoE] n.d.a). It is also the advocated method for EU to eliminating inequalities and promoting equality between men and women in all of its activities, according to the horizontal flanking provision in Article 8 TFEU.

Both the principle of non-discrimination and the gender mainstreaming strategy clearly bind States and other signatory bodies to take action against phenomena that are obstacles to gender equality. The question is then if anti-gender hate speech is an obstacle to achieve gender equality?

It is today clearly declared that anti-gender hate speech does counteract gender equality and also that it may constitute discrimination against women. It may constitute discrimination against women as it may be both gender stereotypical and perceived as violence.

4.3 Specific regulation to combat anti-gender hate speech

4.3.1 UN level

The regulation on discrimination against women on a UN level clearly connects discrimination against women with gender stereotypes and violence against women. Gender stereotypes are condemned in CEDAW Article 5a and that 'States Parties are obliged to take all appropriate measures to modify the social and cultural patterns of conduct of men and women, with a view to achieving the elimination of prejudices and customary and all other practices which are based on the idea of the inferiority or the superiority of either of the sexes or on stereotyped roles for men and women'. The obligation is far-reaching and in line with a transformative understanding of CEDAW (Holtmaat 2013).

Violence against women was recognised as a societal and democratic threat since decades ago. CEDAW, adopted by the General Assembly in 1979, was a crucial instrument. Although men's violence against women is not explicitly addressed in CEDAW, the UN CSW and the Committee on the Elimination of Violence against Women have established that violence against women falls under the prohibition of discrimination of women (Nussbaum 2016). So have the Declaration on the Elimination of Violence against Women, adopted by the UN in 1993, and the Beijing Declaration and Platform for Action of 15 September 1995. Moreover, international criminal law has established that acts of non-physical abuse can constitute sexual violence (de Brouwer 2005; Citron 2009; ICTR in the Akayesu case and ICTY in the Furundzija case).

The United Nations High Commissioner for Human Rights reported to the Human Rights Council about the gendered digital divide (A/HRC/35/9). The divide referred to the measurable gap between women and men in their access to, use of and ability to influence, contribute to and benefit from ICTs. In the report online harassment and violence against women was identified as one of the factors influencing, preventing or inhibiting women's access and use of ICTs.

A year later, in 2018, a special report by the rapporteur addressed online violence against women and girls from a human rights perspective (A/HRC/38/47). Online and ICT-facilitated forms of violence against women have become increasingly common, particularly on social media platforms and other technical applications. When women and girls do have access to and use the Internet, they face online forms and manifestations of violence that are part of the continuum multiple, recurring and interrelated forms of gender-based violence against women. Despite the benefits and empowering potential of the internet and ICT, women and girls across the world have increasingly voiced their concern at harmful, sexist, misogynistic and violent content and behaviour online. It is therefore important to acknowledge that the Internet is being used in a broader environment of widespread and systemic structural discrimination and gender-based violence against women and girls, which frame their access to and use of the Internet and other ICT. Emerging forms of ICT have facilitated new types of gender-based violence and gender inequality in access to technologies, which hinder women's and girls' full enjoyment of their human rights and their ability to achieve gender equality. The States are recommended, among many measures, to enact new laws to prohibit new emerging forms of online gender-based violence (A/HRC/38/47).

The UN agency for gender equality, United Nations Entity for Gender Equality and the Empowerment of Women (UN Women n.d.), which CSW is connected to, was one of the entities within the United Nations Working Group on Hate launched a Strategy and Plan of Action on Hate Speech in 2019. Hate speech is understood as 'any kind of communication in speech, writing or behaviour, that attacks or uses pejorative or discriminatory language with reference to a person or a group on the basis on who they are, in other words, based on their religion, ethnicity, nationality, race, colour, descent, gender or other identity factor. This is often rooted in, and generates intolerance and hatred and, in certain contexts, can be demeaning and divisive' (United Nations 2019).

UN Women informs the Global Partnership for Action on Gender-based Online Harassment and Abuse in 2022.[1] The partnership brings together countries, international organisations, civil society, and the private sector to better prioritise, understand, prevent, and address the growing scourge of technology-facilitated gender-based violence. The Global Partnership is also an action coalition as part of the Denmark-led Technology for Democracy initiative. It will address gender-based online harassment and abuse in the long term, with an initial mission to deliver concrete results. The initial set of member countries in the Global Partnership were United States, Denmark, the United Kingdom, Sweden, Australia, and the Republic of Korea.

UN Women has moreover in 2023 addressed hate speech as one form of technology-facilitated gender-based violence, also including other forms such as cyberbullying, online harassment, doxing, intimate image abuse, trolling, or deep fakes. Technology-facilitated gender-based violence is, according to CSW, a new terminology but not new phenomena. Women, girls, and gender-non-conforming individuals are more likely to be targeted and experience more severe and lasting consequences because of their gender. Studies across the world show that 16–58 per cent of women and girls have been targeted by violence online. The impacts of this type of violence extend beyond the digital sphere, entrenching inequalities and posing a significant threat to women's rights and safety both online and offline (UN Women 2023).

The UN Special Rapporteur on Violence against Women and Girls also declares that women are being subjected to new and emerging forms of violence rooted in misogyny and patriarchy, exercised online and offline and negatively impacting all spheres of life thereby not only affecting their lives, safety, dignity, and freedom, but their equal and full participation in society as a whole. Participation is crucial in a democracy, as is a presence of a diversity of voices. The UN Special Rapporteur calls on States to strongly consider the adoption of an optional protocol on violence against women to the CEDAW (Special Statement by Current and Former Special Rapporteurs on Violence against Women, Its Causes and Consequences 2023).

4.3.2 *European level*

The most comprehensive legally binding document when it comes to violence against women in Europe is the Council of Europe's Convention on Preventing and Combating Violence against Women and Domestic Violence from 2014, also known as 'the Istanbul Convention' (CETS no. 210, 2011). It requires parties to develop laws, policies and support services to end violence against women and domestic violence (Art. 7). It adopts a transformative perception of equality (Art. 12). It is not only the States that are required to take action but also private sector, the information and communication technology sector and the media. They are all required to participate in the elaboration and implementation of policies and to set guidelines and self-regulatory standards to prevent violence against women and to enhance respect for their dignity (Art. 17). State Parties shall take the necessary legislative or other measures to ensure that the intentional conduct of repeatedly engaging in threatening conduct directed at another person, causing her or him to fear for her or his safety, is criminalised (Art. 34). The same requirements are there to ensure that any form of unwanted verbal, non-verbal or physical conduct of a sexual nature with the purpose or effect of violating the dignity of a person, in particular when creating an intimidating, hostile, degrading, humiliating or offensive environment, is subject to criminal or other legal sanction (Art. 40). The convention certainly puts pressure on the State Parties to take action.

The Group of Experts on Action against Violence against Women and Domestic Violence (GREVIO) monitors the implementation of the Istanbul Convention. It covers in its monitoring online sexual harassment, online and technology-facilitated stalking, and the digital dimension of psychological violence – all relevant in the context of combating sexist hate speech targeting women.

The Council has declared that sexist hate speech online and offline is a daily phenomenon for many women that is not very visible and only beginning to be addressed. It was in 2015 that sex and gender was included in the definition of hate speech for the first time (Recommendation no. 15). Some groups of women are particularly targeted by sexist hate speech for example young women, women of colour, women politicians or feminist activists. The Council of Europe has moreover raised the importance of combating hate speech through its work on gender equality and through standards: the 2015 and 2022 Recommendations on Hate Speech (Recommendation no. 15 from 2015; Recommendation CM/Rec(2022)16, Combating Sexist Hate Speech 2016, a recommendation on preventing and combating sexism from 2019[2]), accompanied by a campaign 'Sexism: See it. Name it. Stop it!, with tools available in different languages (CoE 2020). The 2019 Recommendation declares that the need to tackle *sexist speech*, among other types of sexism, is implicit in a number of international and regional instruments.

The Council of Europe monitors an extensive body of work on hate speech (CoE n.d.b). The used definition of hate speech within this body is with a reference to the Recommendation CM/Rec(2022)16(1) of the Committee of Ministers to member States on combating hate speech:

> All types of expression that incite, promote, spread or justify violence, hatred or discrimination against a person or group of persons, or that denigrates them, by reason of their real or attributed personal characteristics or status such as 'race',[3] colour, language, religion, nationality, national or ethnic origin, age, disability, sex, gender identity and sexual orientation.

The definition is almost the same as in the previous General Policy Recommendation no. 15.

The Council of Europe's Gender Equality Strategy for 2024–2029 (CM(2024)17-final) points at the backsliding on gender equality policies and the rise of anti-gender movements. Anti-gender and gender-critical narratives are, according to the Council, often used as a tool to promote a broader agenda of opposing gender equality and women's rights. The fight for gender equality must challenge this anti-gender trend as such.

Anti-rights movements seek to roll back progress on human rights and maintain the status quo of discrimination and inequality. They use various tactics to undermine rights, including spreading misinformation and disinformation, promoting hateful rhetoric and pushing for regressive policies. This backsliding is reflected in the intensification of sexist hate speech in Europe, especially online. Discrimination and sexist hate speech provide fertile ground for violence against women and girls, which is one of the most serious human rights violations suffered by women and girls. Women also face more restrictions and harassment aiming to silence women human rights defenders and persons who defend women's rights. The response of national authorities, including the police, prosecutors and judges, as well as health personnel, is often inadequate in cases of violence against women and girls and must be strengthened (CoE 2024).

The Council has sharpened its wordings on anti-gender hate speech sine the previous two Gender equality strategies. In the strategy for the years 2014–2017 (CoE 2014) it was explicitly stated, under its strategic objective 1 – combating gender stereotypes and sexism, that *sexist hate speech must be tackled.* The urgency to take action against sexist hate speech online and offline was repeated in the following gender equality strategies for 2018–2023 (CoE 2018), under the strategic objective 1 – to prevent and combat gender stereotypes and sexism. The Council has continued to address hate speech as a form of sexism, analyse and monitor its impact, in co-operation with other relevant sectors of the Council of Europe.

What becomes clear in the three mentioned gender equality strategies is that the view on anti-gender hate speech over time has been sharpened, from considered as gender stereotypical to a form of violence against women. What is also clear is that the phenomenon increasingly is seen as one form of violence connected to other forms. Both the Istanbul Convention and CEDAW recognise a continuum between gender stereotypes, gender inequality, sexism and violence against women and girls. In this way, acts of everyday sexism in the form of apparently inconsequential or minor sexist behaviour, comments and jokes are at one end of the continuum. These acts are moreover declared as humiliating and contributing to a social climate where women are demeaned, their self-regard lowered and their activities and choices restricted, including at work, in the private, public or online sphere. Sexist hate speech may escalate to or incite overtly offensive and threatening acts, including sexual abuse or violence, rape or potentially lethal action. Other consequences may include loss of resources, self-harm or suicide. Tackling sexism is thus, according to the Council of Europe, 'part of States' positive obligation to guarantee human rights, gender equality and to prevent violence against women and girls in accordance with international human rights law and, for States Parties, the Istanbul Convention' (Recommendation CM/Rec(2019)1).

The EU legal framework is obviously founded on the principles of equality and non-discrimination and supports international conventions such as CEDAW and the Istanbul Convention. Statements and legislation on combating violence against women and domestic violence, and against trafficking in human beings and sexual exploitation, in particular women and children, has been adopted based on Articles 82 and 83 TFEU.[4] But when it comes to more specific targets against hate speech as a form of hate crime the situation has been fragmented and not including gender until recently. The Council Framework Decision 2008/913/JHA of 28 November 2008 on combating certain forms and expressions of racism and xenophobia by means of criminal law criminalised hate speech and hate crime against a group of persons or a member of such a group based on race, colour, religion, descent or national or ethnic origin'. The European Parliament Briefing 'Hate Speech and Hate Crime: Time to Act?' from September 2024 declared that

> over the last 20 years, there has been a marked increase in hate speech and hate crime in Europe. Expressing hate has become socially acceptable, stigmatising and dehumanising individuals and groups of people for characteristics ranging from age, ethnicity, gender identity, language, nationality, race, religion, and sex to sexual orientation. Widespread use of the internet and social media has increasingly brought hate speech online.

Moreover, it was clarified that whereas all EU Member States have criminalised hate speech based on the grounds covered by the 2008 framework decision, national laws differ with regard to other protected characteristics, such as gender, disability, sexual orientation and age, for example (European Parliament 2024). A recently adopted directive, the EU Directive 2024/1385, now requires Member States to criminalise hate speech against women alongside other forms of gender-based cyber-violence. Article 8 of the directive requires Member States to make it a crime to intentionally incite violence or hatred against a group of persons or a member of such a group, defined by reference to gender, by publicly disseminating material containing incitement online.

The purpose of this Directive is

> to provide a comprehensive framework to effectively prevent and combat violence against women and domestic violence throughout the Union.

> It does so by strengthening and introducing measures in relation to the following areas: the definition of relevant criminal offences and penalties, the protection of victims and access to justice, victim support, enhanced data collection, prevention, coordination and cooperation.
>
> (Recital 1)

In Recital 25 the directive declares:

> Over recent years, the increase in internet and social media usage has led to a sharp rise in public incitement to violence and hatred, including based on gender. The easy, fast and broad sharing of hate speech through the digital world is reinforced by the online disinhibition effect, as presumed anonymity on the internet and a sense of impunity reduces people's inhibition to engage in such speech. Women are often the target of sexist and misogynous hate online, which can escalate into hate crime offline. That conduct needs to be prevented or intercepted at an early stage. The language used in that type of incitement does not always directly refer to the gender of the targeted person, but the biased motivation can be inferred from the overall content or context of the incitement.

The Member States shall bring into force the laws, regulations and administrative provisions necessary to comply with the Directive by 14 June 2027. This directive is thoroughly discussed by Öberg (2024), concluding that it appears that the EU is conducting recently a more markedly 'expressive' and value-based approach to criminalisation, taking a stand against certain conduct even if it has no significant cross-border dimension. The EU's actions reflect a need to reinforce the Union's fundamental values, demonstrating a commitment to human rights and equality.

There have also been intergovernmental activities among Member States of the EU. For example, Sweden has together with Luxembourg partly funded a project implemented by the UNDP Funding Window for Governance, Peacebuilding, Crisis and Resilience, 'Promoting Dialogue and Joint Action to Combat Hate Speech' (UNDP 2023).

4.3.3 National level

4.3.3.1 Sweden

The principle of equal rights between men and women is expressed in the Swedish constitution since 1976. It has been criticised as it has mainly been interpreted in a formal way, despite the fact that the constitution has opened for a substantive or even transformative application. This possibility has however been reduced over time (Svensson & Gunnarsson 2012; Gunnarsson, Svenaeus & Svensson 2024). The driving force for gender equality in Sweden has mainly been the gender equality policy, underpinned by the idea that 'women and men shall have the same power to shape society and their own lives' (Gender Equality Policy in Sweden 2024). This overarching goal has six sub-goals expressing aspects that are of specific importance in achieving the gender equality goal.[5] Here, the sixth is of most interest, Preventing and combating men's violence against women. It has been extended, and today it also includes sexual offence legislation based on consent as well as combating prostitution and trafficking in human beings for the purpose of sexual exploitation. Even though anti-gender hate speech is not explicitly addressed, the 'fight against all forms of sexual and gender-based violence both offline and online is an important goal in Sweden's development cooperation' is declared (Gender Equality Policy in Sweden 2024). Moreover, under the first sub-goal, Gender-equal division of power and influence, it is stated that 'preventing and counteracting gendered and sexist violence, threats and hatred against elected officials and journalists online and offline is a priority issue for Sweden' (Gender Equality Policy in Sweden 2024; see also Niemi-Kiesiläinen 2006).

Even though the gender equality policy might be interpreted as if online anti-gender hate speech is targeted, the regulation and measures against 'hate speech' and 'hate crimes'[6] do not cover gender. The corresponding regulation is fragmented (Bladini 2020; see Chapter 6). The national action programme against racism, xenophobia, homophobia and discrimination (Skr. 2000/01: 59), updated in 2016 and in 2022, resulting in five action programmes against Afrophobia, Antisemitism, Anti-ziganism, Islamophobia and the Sámi group (Samlat grepp mot rasism och hatbrott), confirms this picture. A new updated programme is under development, but there are no signs of including hate crimes against women or based on gender (Regeringen stärker arbetet mot rasism och hatbrott 2024).

The 2015 national strategy against men's violence against women (SOU 2015: 55), running for 10 years 2016–2025, had as its mission to suggest a comprehensive national strategy to reach the gender equality sub-goal about ending men's violence against women. References are made to international legal instruments like the Bill of rights, CEDAW and the Commission supervising the convention, the 1993 Declaration on the Elimination of Violence against Women, the statement by the Special Rapporteur statement in 1993 at the world conference in Vienna that violence against women is an violation of women's human rights, the Beijing platform, several initiatives taken by the organisation UN Women and other initiatives taken by UN to counteract violence against women (SOU 2015: 55, pp. 183–188). In addition, references are made also to WHO's resolution WHA 56.24 to the Child Convention of 1989 (CRC). In addition, references are also made to European human rights instruments such as ECHR, the Istanbul Convention as well as the EU directive on victims from 2012 (2012/29/EU). When Sweden is in the strategy compared to other countries, it is declared that Sweden does well, even though the focus has been on criminal law means.

Means to counteract anti-gender hate speech shines however with its absence in the 2015 strategy, although the strategy states that girls and women are exposed to violence in all spheres of life, also on the internet (SOU 2015: 55, p. 52). Especially violence directed against girls and young women are exposed to psychological violence, constraint, pressure and control via digital and social media (SOU 2015: 55, p. 154). It is moreover focused on men's participation and responsibility; strategic, cohesive and long-term agency governance; and it includes the task of reviewing the regulation of sexual abuse and the regulations of sexual crimes online.

A Committee on the democratic conversation in a digital age (SOU 2020: 56) had a focus on how to promote individual and societal resilience towards disinformation, propaganda and online hate speech. One way to go is to raise the participation in democracy. Thus, one of the goals of freedom of expression, to guarantee a diversity of voices, is seen as essential. The access to the internet and social media platforms is assessed as important and as something that might have increased the participation in manifestations in civil society. At the same time, digitalisation has consequences like exclusion of individuals and groups that don't have access to digital tools, such as older, low educated, low income people etc. Another consequence is online hate directed towards individuals and groups. Themes that trigger especially strong reactions are, according to the Committee, gender equality and feminism, discrimination, religion, racism, integration, migration, immigration and climate/environment (SOU 2020: 56, p. 95).

Moreover, the Committee claims that online hate has consequences for individuals and for the society. Online hate directed against elected officials, and groups of certain importance in a democracy such as journalists, researchers just to mention some, challenges the essence of a democracy. Also, online hate directed at women and people with foreign background seriously affects the democratic society. The risk is that individuals exposed to online hate cease to take part in the conversation. But also other persons, not yet taking part in the conversation, might feel afraid to take part. Thus, democracy is undermined (SOU 2020: 56, pp. 101–103).

One of the authorities mentioned as a contributor to a strengthened resilience against the negative consequences is the Swedish Press and Broadcasting Authority (*Myndigheten för press, radio och tv*). They have as their task to work to promote freedom of expression and support the possibilities to a diversity of voices and availability within press and broadcasting. Also, the Police Authority's responsibility to inform the public about the necessity of reporting threat, hate and violence (SOU 2020: 56, p. 127). However, when the hate is directed against women it is not always illegal, contrary to what is the case when the hate is based on racism or sexuality. Despite this, the Committee suggests nothing but a strategy for increased resilience against disinformation, propaganda and online hate.

Another Committee on democracy (SOU 2022: 28), formulated three objectives for its work. In summary, these were to increase the number of people who have a good knowledge of democracy, the number of people who are involved in democracy and the number who take a clear stance in favour of the democratic system of governance (SOU 2022: 28, p. 31). The means suggested and performed during the Committees' term of office were mainly knowledge information and opinion formation.

The Swedish Agency for the Media (from 2024 *Mediemyndigheten*, previously the Swedish Media Council/*Statens Medieråd*) was in 2021 given a mission by the Government to identify and compile methods to counteract racism, and similar forms of hostility and hate crimes directed against children and young persons on the internet (*Att motverka rasism, annan fientlighet och hatbrott på nätet bland barn och unga: En kunskapsöversikt* 2021). The mission is a part of the national action programme against racism, xenophobia, homophobia and discrimination, mentioned above, and connected to the No Hate Speech movement, an initiative taken by the European Council in 2013. The mission focuses on raising awareness among children and young people about racism and similar hostilities online. It also aims to strengthen children and young people's ability to use their freedom of expression and to respect human rights and equality as well as stimulate critical thinking when using social media. Hostilities online based on sex/gender was however not included in the mission and in the report.

There is a Swedish strategy to combat terrorism and the work against violent extremism (Skr. 2023/24: 56). This report refers to a research overview (CVE 2022) and addresses the anti-gender attitude within the extreme right movements, especially in terms of ideals of masculinity and the women's role in families. It highlights the problem that right-wing extremists are questioning gender perspectives and recognising them as a threat to democracy. Misogyny is central in these movements and connected to conservative perceptions of men and women as essentially different and devoted to different roles in society and in activism. Misogyny might appear in various expressions but has often to do with control of women's sexuality and about (re)establishing men's power and superiority in public and private life. The extreme movement are dominated by men and violence is used to claim male status. The report identifies connections between ideologically motivated violence and violence in intimate relationships. The work to prevent the glorification of violence in the extreme movements and in terrorism has thus importance for preventing men's violence against women (Skr. 2023/24: 56, p. 9).

The Swedish government adopted an Action Programme against Men's Violence against Women, Domestic Violence and Honour-Based Violence and Oppression in June 2024. It expresses an ambition to increase the professional knowledge of digital violence, or digital dimensions of violence. Such violence includes sexual harassment, stalking, psychological violence and attempts to contact children under the age of 18 online for sexual purposes. The government aims to gather existing knowledge from the public sector, non-governmental organisations and the business sector to strengthen action against digital violence, in this area, as well as develop new measures to prevent digital dimensions of violence (Action Programme against Men's Violence against Women, Domestic Violence and Honour-Based Violence and Oppression 2024).

4.3.3.2 Italy

In Italy, there is a notable absence of specific legislation addressing discrimination based on gender, gender identity, or sexual orientation. The current anti-discrimination criminal laws are exclusively focused on biases related to race, ethnicity, nationality, or religion.

The Italian Constitution, which entered into force on 1st January 1948, was introduced as a reaction to a dramatic past characterised by violence and discrimination (D'Amico & Siccardi 2021), as demonstrated by the articles n°2[7] and n°3[8], which recognise and guarantee the inviolable rights of the person, as well as the dignity and equality of each and every person.

Because of these articles, it would be the legislator's responsibility to combat inequality and discrimination, whatever their nature or their causes may be (Commissione straordinaria per il contrasto dei fenomeni di intolleranza, razzismo, antisemitismo e istigazione all'odio e alla violenza 2022). However, equality is neither mentioned in terms of gender nor of gender identity, but only in terms of sex, race, political opinion, personal and social condition.

Regarding reforms, the ECRI (European Commission against Racism and Intolerance), in its sixth report on Italy published on 22nd October 2024 (ECRI 2024), 'requests that the authorities take action in a number of areas and makes a series of recommendations' (p. 6). In this report, ECRI highlights that 'the public discourse has become increasingly xenophobic and political speech has taken on highly divisive and antagonistic overtones particularly targeting refugees, asylum seekers and migrants, as well as Italian citizens with migrant backgrounds, Roma and LGBTI persons' (p. 15) and that hate speech 'often remains unchallenged' (p. 5).

4.3.3.3 Spain

The most significant legislation on gender equality in Spain is Organic Law 3/2007, of 22nd March, on effective equality between women and men. While the law does not address anti-gender hate speech or discrimination in the digital context, it defines both direct and indirect discrimination on the grounds of sex, as well as sexual harassment as a form of direct discrimination.

4.4 Concluding remarks

The extensive body of international and national regulation on gender equality taken together, gives a very clear and consistent position, namely that *anti-gender hate speech counteracts gender equality* on an individual basis as well as on a societal level.

Individually it takes the shape of physical and psychological threats and violence which causes harm and fear and as a consequence may lead to silenced voices. If so, the consequences are also societal. Silenced voices result in a democratic deficiency and are contradictory to the democratic value anchored in the justifications of freedom of expressions as a common good, requiring a diversity of voices. If the silencing has a gendered bias, the consequences are also contradictory to the goal of gender equality. Thus, the connection between gender equality, freedom of expression as a means to safeguard democracy and anti-gender hate speech is clear. What is also clear is that the ambition to counteract anti-gender hate speech has over time become more urgent and expressed by so many actors and bodies on international, regional and national levels.

It is therefore surprising or even astonishing that, still, the problem is handled in such a fragmented way and rarely in line with hate speech based on other grounds than sex/gender. This goes especially on the national level, taking Sweden as an example. The commonly used explanation for the hesitance, a reluctance to intervene in the essential democratic element of freedom of expression, is, as we have argued doubtful given two aspects. First, freedom of exoression requires also a diversity of voices. Second, anti-gender hate speech is a form of violence agianst women and counteracts the goal of gender equality.

Notes

1 The webpage for the partnership is no longer available at the U.S Department of State site. We presume that this has to do with the new presidency. USA was part of it from the beginning, see www.government.se/statements/2024/09/global-partnership-statement-on-gendered-disinformation/ but not anymore, see www.diplomatie.gouv.fr/en/french-foreign-policy/digital-diplomacy/news/article/the-global-partnership-for-action-on-gender-based-online-harassment-and-abuse.

2 In a previous document from 2015 the scope of what was considered hate speech was restricted to discrimination against lesbian, gay, bisexual and transgender persons, Recommendation CM/Rec (2010)5 on measures to combat discrimination on grounds of sexual orientation or gender identity.

3 In the document, the term 'race' is used in order to ensure that those persons who are generally and erroneously perceived as 'belonging to another race' are not excluded from the protection provided for by the legislation and the implementation of policies to prevent and combat hate speech. See footnote to art. 2. CM/Rec(2022)16.

4 See, e.g., European Parliament (2022) and Directive (EU) 2024/1385 of the European Parliament and of the Council of 14 May 2024 on combating violence against women and domestic violence, OJ L, 24.5.2024.

5 The subgoals are (1) gender-equal division of power and influence; (2) economic gender equality; (3) gender-equal education; (4) an equal distribution of unpaid housework and provision of care work; (5) gender-equal health; and (6) preventing and combating men's violence against women (Gender Equality Policy in Sweden 2024).

6 Neither hate speech nor hate crimes are Swedish legal terms.
7 The Constitution of the Italian Republic recognises and guarantees the inviolable rights of the person, both as an individual and in the social groups where human personality is expressed. The Republic expects that the fundamental duties of political, economic and social solidarity be fulfilled.
8 All citizens have equal social dignity and are equal before the law, without distinction of sex, race, language, religion, political opinion, personal and social conditions. It is the duty of the Constitution of the Italian Republic to remove those obstacles of an economic or social nature which constrain the freedom and equality of citizens, thereby impeding the full development of the human person and the effective participation of all workers in the political, economic and social organisation of the country.

References

Literature

Bladini, M. (2020), 'Silenced voices. Online violence targeting women as a threat to democracy', *Nordic Journal on Law and Society*, 3(2), 1–42.
Center mot våldsbejakande extremism (CVE) (2022). https://cve.se/publikationer/manmaskulinitetochvaldsbejakandeextremismenkunskapsoversikt.5.11258e6a184d17a7b2ca1b.html.
Citron, D. K. (2009), 'Law's expressive value in combating cyber gender harassment', *Michigan Law Review*, 108(3), 373–415.
D'Amico, M. & Siccardi, C. (Eds.) (2021), *La Costituzione non odia. Conoscere, prevenire e contrastare l'hate speech on line*. Giappichelli.
De Brouwer, A.-M. (2005), 'Supranatural criminal prosecution of sexual violence'. In Durham, H. & Gurd, T. (Eds.), *Listening to the silences: Women and war*. Brill.
Gunnarsson, Å., Svenaeus, L. & Svensson, E.-M. (2024), 'Sweden: From proactive policies to anti-discrimination law'. In Hellum, A., Ikdahl, I., Blaker Strand, V. & Svensson, E-M. (Eds.), *Nordic equality and anti-discrimination laws in the throes of change: Legal developments in Sweden, Finland, Norway, and Iceland*. Taylor & Francis. https://doi.org/10.4324/9781003172840.
Holtmaat, H. M. T. (2013), 'CEDAW: A holistic approach to women's equality and freedom'. In Hellum, A. & Sinding-Aasen H. S. (Eds.), *Women's human rights: CEDAW in international, regional and national law*. Cambridge University Press.
Niemi-Kiesiläinen, J. (2006), 'Feminist policy against violence in Sweden'. In Bondesson, U.V. (Ed.), *Law & morality*. Forlaget Thomson A/S
Nussbaum, M. C. (2016), 'Women's progress and women's human rights', *Human Rights Quarterly*, 38(3), 589–622. https://doi.org/10.1353/hrq.2016.0043.
Öberg, J. (2024), *The normative foundations for EU criminal justice. Powers, limits and justifications*. Hart.
Svensson, E.-M. (2021), 'Law and governance'. In *Pan-Arctic report*. Gender Equality in the Arctic.
Svensson, E.-M. & Gunnarsson, Å. (2012), 'Gender equality in the welfare state', *feminists@law*, 2(1), 1–27.

Court cases

The International Criminal Tribunal for Rwanda (ICTR)

Prosecutor v. Akayesu. Case No. ICTR-96-4-T. Judgment 688. International Criminal Tribunal for Rwanda, 2 Sept. 1998.

The International Criminal Tribunal for Former Yugoslavia (ICTY)

Prosecutor v Furundzija. Case No. IT-95-17/1-T. Judgment 186. International Criminal Tribunal for Former Yugoslavia, 10 Dec. 1998.

Public documents and laws

International (UN)

A/76/258 (2021), *Promotion and protection of the right to freedom of opinion and expression*. United Nations General Assembly. Note by the Secretary-General.

A/HRC/35/9 (2017), *Promotion, protection and enjoyment of human rights on the Internet: ways to bridge the gender digital divide from a human rights perspective*. Human Rights Council.

A/HRC/38/47 (2018), *Report of the Special Rapporteur on violence against women, its causes and consequences on online violence against women and girls from a human rights perspective*. United Nations General Assembly. Note by the Secretariat. https://documents-dds-ny.un.org/doc/UNDOC/GEN/G18/184/58/PDF/G1818458.pdf?OpenElement (accessed 2024-10-23).

Beijing Declaration and Platform for Action: 4th World Conference on Women, Beijing, China, 4–15 September 1995. https://digitallibrary.un.org/record/1648092?ln=en (accessed 2024-12-01).

Convention on the Elimination of All Forms of Discrimination against Women (CEDAW), New York, 18 Dec. 1979, entered into force 3 Sep. 1981. www.ohchr.org/sites/default/files/cedaw.pdf (accessed 2024-10-23).

Convention on the Rights of the Child (CRC), New York, 20 Nov. 1989, entered into force 2 Sep. 1990. www.ohchr.org/sites/default/files/crc.pdf (accessed 2024-10-23).

Declaration on the Elimination of Violence against Women, Proclaimed by General Assembly Resolution 48/104 of 20 December 1993. www.ohchr.org/sites/default/files/eliminationvaw.pdf (accessed 2024-09-03).

ECOSOC (1997), *Gender mainstreaming*, A/52/3. www.un.org/womenwatch/daw/csw/GMS.PDF (accessed 2024-10-31).

Global Partnership for Action on Gender-Based Online Harassment and Abuse (2022). www.diplomatie.gouv.fr/en/french-foreign-policy/digital-diplomacy/news/article/the-global-partnership-for-action-on-gender-based-online-harassment-and-abuse/ (accessed 2024-11-26).

International Covenant on Civil and Political Rights (ICCPR), New York, 16 Dec. 1966, entered into force 23 Mar. 1976, the provisions of article 41, entered into force 28 Mar. 1979. Human Rights Committee. www.ohchr.org/sites/default/files/ccpr.pdf (accessed 2024-10-23).

International Covenant on Economic, Social and Cultural Rights (ICESCR), New York, 16 Dec. 1966, entered into force 3 Jan. 1976. www.ohchr.org/sites/default/files/cescr.pdf (accessed 2024-10-23).

Special Statement by Current and Former Special Rapporteurs on Violence against Women, Its Causes and Consequences (2023), Now *is the time for an optional protocol to CEDAW on violence against women and girls*. United Nations Human Rights Special Procedures. www.ohchr.org/sites/default/files/documents/issues/women/sr/statements/stm-op-vaw-sr-vaw-7-12-23.pdf (accessed 2024-09-02).

Transforming Our World: The 2030 Agenda for Sustainable Development (2015), *A/RES/70/1*. United Nations General Assembly Resolution adopted on 25 September 2015. https://documents.un.org/doc/undoc/gen/n15/291/89/pdf/n1529189.pdf (accessed 2024-10-23).

UN Development Programme (UNDP) (2023), 'United in the fight against sexism, misogyny, and gender-based hate speech'. www.undp.org/montenegro/news/united-fight-against-sexism-misogyny-and-gender-based-hate-speech (accessed 2024-10-23).

UN Women (2023), 'Creating safe digital spaces free of trolls, doxing, and hate speech'. www.unwomen.org/en/news-stories/explainer/2023/11/creating-safe-digital-spaces-free-of-trolls-doxing-and-hate-speech (accessed 2024-11-26).

UN Women (n.d.), 'UN agency for gender equality and the empowerment of women'. www.un.org/youthenvoy/2013/07/un-women-the-united-nations-entity-for-gender-equality-and-the-empowerment-of-women/ (accessed 2024-11-26).

United Nations (2019), 'UN strategy and plan of action on hate speech'. www.un.org/en/genocideprevention/documents/UN%20Strategy%20and%20Plan%20of%20Action%20on%20Hate%20Speech%2018%20June%20SYNOPSIS.pdf (accessed 2024-10-23).

Universal Declaration of Human Rights (UDHR) (10 Dec. 1948), U.N.G.A. Res. 217 A (III) (1948). www.ohchr.org/en/human-rights/universal-declaration/translations/english (accessed 2024-10-23).

World Health Organization, Resolution WHA 56.24, 'Implementing the recommendations of the World Report on Violence and Health'. https://apps.who.int/gb/ebwha/pdf_files/WHA56/ea56r24.pdf (accessed 2024-11-27).

International (Council of Europe and EU)

Committee of Ministers (2022), 'Recommendation CM/Rec(2022)16 20/05/22 of the Committee of Ministers to member States on combating hate speech'. www.coe.int/en/web/combating-hate-speech/recommendation-on-combating-hate-speech (accessed 2024-10-24).

Council of Europe (CoE) (2010), 'Recommendation CM/Rec(2010)5 of the Committee of Ministers to member states on measures to combat discrimination on grounds of sexual orientation or gender identity'. ww.coe.int/en/web/sogi/rec-2010-5 (accessed 2024-12-01).

Council of Europe (CoE) (2011), Convention on Preventing and Combating Violence against Women and Domestic Violence (Istanbul Convention, CETS no. 210). www.coe.int/en/web/istanbul-convention/text-of-the-convention (accessed 2024-10-23).

Council of Europe (CoE) (2014), *Gender equality strategy 2014–2017*. https://rm.coe.int/1680590174 (accessed 2024-10-23).

Council of Europe (CoE) (2016), *Combating sexist hate speech*. www.coe.int/en/web/genderequality/sexist-hate-speech#%7B%22635583504%22:[1]%7D (accessed 2024-09-02).

Council of Europe (CoE) (2018), *Gender equality strategy 2018–2023*. https://rm.coe.int/prems-093618-gbr-gender-equality-strategy-2023-web-a5/16808b47el (accessed 2024-10-23).

Council of Europe (CoE) (2019), Preventing and Combating Sexism, Recommendation CM/Rec(2019)1, adopted by the Committee of Ministers of the Council of Europe 27 March 2019. https://rm.coe.int/ge-strategy-2018-2023/1680791246 (accessed 2025-02-12).

Council of Europe (CoE) (2020), 'Sexism: See it, Name it, Stop it!' https://rm.coe.int/brochure-sexism/16809fba84 (accessed 2024-09-02).

Council of Europe (CoE) (2024), *Gender equality strategy 2024–2029* (CM(2024)17-final). https://rm.coe.int/prems-073024-gbr-2573-gender-equality-strategy-2024-29-txt-web-a5-2756/1680afc66a (accessed 2024-10-23).

Council of Europe (CoE) (n.d.a), 'Gender mainstreaming at the Council of Europe'. www.coe.int/en/web/genderequality/gender-mainstreaming (accessed 2024-10-31).

Council of Europe (CoE) (n.d.b), 'Combating hate speech'. www.coe.int/en/web/combating-hate-speech (accessed 2024-10-23).

Council Framework Decision 2008/913/JHA of 28 November 2008 on combating certain forms and expressions of racism and xenophobia by means of criminal law (the 2008 Council Framework Decision). https://eur-lex.europa.eu/legal-content/EN/TXT/PDF/?uri=CELEX:32008F0913 (accessed 2024-10-31).

Directive 2012/29/EU of the European Parliament and of the Council of 25 October 2012 establishing minimum standards on the rights, support and protection of victims of crime, and replacing Council Framework Decision 2001/220/JHA. https://eur-lex.europa.eu/legal-content/EN/TXT/PDF/?uri=CELEX:32012L0029 (accessed 2024-10-24).

Directive (EU) 2024/1385 of the European Parliament and of the Council of 14 May 2024 on combating violence against women and domestic violence. https://eur-lex.europa.eu/legal-content/EN/TXT/?uri=OJ%3AL_202401385 (accessed 2024-10-23).

ECRI (2024), Report on Italy (sixth monitoring cycle), Council of Europe, Adopted on 2 July 2024 Published on 22 October 2024. https://rm.coe.int/sixth-ecri-report-on-italy/1680b205f5 (accessed 2024-12-01).

European Commission against Racism and Intolerance (ECRI) (2015), General Policy Recommendation no 15 on Combating Hate Speech Adopted on 8 December 2015. https://rm.coe.int/ecri-general-policy-recommendation-no-15-on-combating-hate-speech/16808b5b01 (accessed 2024-10-23).

European Convention on Human Rights (ECHR). www.echr.coe.int/documents/convention_eng.pdf (accessed 2024-10-23).

European Parliament (2022), European Parliament resolution of 14 December 2021 with recommendations to the Commission on combating gender-based violence: cyberviolence (2020/2035(INL)). https://eur-lex.europa.eu/legal-content/EN/TXT/PDF/?uri=CELEX:52021IP0489 (accessed 2024-10-23).

European Parliament (2024a), 'The Parliament's fight for gender equality in the EU'. www.europarl.europa.eu/news/en/headlines/priorities/social/20190712STO56961/the-parliament-s-fight-for-gender-equality-in-the-eu (accessed 2024-10-23).

European Parliament (2024b), 'Hate speech and hate crime: Time to act?' www.europarl.europa.eu/RegData/etudes/BRIE/2024/762389/EPRS_BRI(2024)762389_EN.pdf (accessed 2024-10-31).

Group of Experts on Action against Violence against Women and Domestic Violence (GREVIO), General Recommendation no. 1 on the digital dimension of violence against women adopted on 20 October 2021. https://rm.coe.int/grevio-rec-no-on-digital-violence-against-women/1680a49147 (accessed 2024-10-23).

Protocol No. 12 to the Convention for the Protection of Human Rights and Fundamental Freedoms Rome, 4.XI.2000. www.echr.coe.int/documents/d/echr/convention_ENG (accessed 2024-10-29).

Sweden

Action Programme against Men's Violence against Women, Domestic Violence and Honour-Based Violence and Oppression (2024). www.government.se/press-releases/2024/06/action-programme-against-mens-violence-against-women-intimate-partner-violence-and-honour-based-violence-and-oppression/ (accessed 2024-08-30).

Att motverka rasism, annan fientlighet och hatbrott på nätet bland barn och unga: En kunskapsöversikt (2021), Slutredovisning av Regeringsuppdrag A2021/00972, Statens medieråd. https://mediemyndigheten.se/globalassets/rapporter-och-analyser/2023/att-motverka-rasism_rapport_tillganglighetsanpassad.pdf (accessed 2024-10-24).

Gender Equality Policy in Sweden (2024). www.government.se/information-material/2019/03/gender-equality-policy-in-sweden/ (accessed 2024-08-30).

NoHate (n.d.), 'No hate speech youth movement campaign'. www.nohate.se/ (accessed 2024-11.27).

Regeringen stärker arbetet mot rasism och hatbrott (2024). www.regeringen.se/pressmeddelanden/2024/03/regeringen-starker-arbetet-mot-rasism-och-hatbrott (accessed 2024-11-27).

Samlat grepp mot rasism och hatbrott. www.regeringen.se/regeringens-politik/samlat-grepp-mot-rasism-och-hatbrott/ (accessed 2024-11-27).

Skr. 2000/01: 59, *En nationell handlingsplan mot rasism, främlingsfientlighet, homofobi och diskriminering.* https://data.riksdagen.se/fil/2f77ab3c-37b5-4ce1-95f0-acc693291b9d (accessed 2024-11-27).

Skr. 2023/24: 56, *Nationell strategi mot våldsbejakande extremism och terrorism – förebygga, förhindra, skydda och hantera.* www.regeringen.se/contentassets/e30421686167432d87cfb77fbe2a6dad/nationell-strategi-mot-valdsbejakande-extremism-och-terrorism--forebygga-forhindra-skydda-och-hantera-skr-20232456/ (accessed 2024-11-27).

SOU 2015: 55, *Nationell strategi mot mäns våld mot kvinnor och hedersrelaterat våld och förtryck*, Slutbetänkande av Utredningen som ska föreslå en nationell strategi mot mäns våld mot kvinnor, Elanders Sverige AB. www.regeringen.se/contentassets/738becd6961e4a3d8d986c00b8c8bc9e/nationell-strategi-mot-mans-vald-mot-kvinnor-och-hedersrelaterat-vald-och-fortryck-sou_2015_55.pdf (accessed 2024-11-27).

SOU 2020: 56, *Det demokratiska samtalet i en digital tid Så stärker vi motståndskraften mot desinformation, propaganda och näthat*. Betänkande av kommittén Nationell satsning på medie- och informationskunnighet och det demokratiska samtalet. Elanders Sverige AB, 2020. www.regeringen.se/contentassets/ffa5b8002c4c4913b063bc5862d6fb48/det-demokratiska-samtalet-i-en-digital-tid---sa-starker-vi-motstandskraften-mot-desinformation-propaganda-och-nathat-sou-202056.pdf (accessed 2024-11-27).

SOU 2022: 28, *Vår demokrati – värd att värna varje dag*. Betänkande av kommittén Demokratin 100 år – samling för en stark demokrati. Elanders Sverige AB, Stockholm 2022. www.regeringen.se/rattsliga-dokument/statens-offentliga-utredningar/2022/06/sou-202228/ (accessed 2024-11-27).

Other sources

Commission on the Status of Women (CSW) (n.d.). www.unwomen.org/en/how-we-work/commission-on-the-status-of-women (accessed 2024-10-23).

Commissione straordinaria per il contrasto dei fenomeni di intolleranza, razzismo, antisemitismo e istigazione all'odio e alla violenza (2022), *Report a conclusione dell'indagine conoscitiva su natura, cause e sviluppi recenti del fenomeno dei discorsi d'odio, con particolare attenzione all'evoluzione della normativa europea in materia*. Senato della Repubblica Italiana. www.senato.it/service/PDF/PDFServer/DF/410798.pdf (accessed 2024-11-28).

Constitution of the Italian Republic, Senato della Repubblica. www.senato.it/documenti/repository/istituzione/costituzione_inglese.pdf (accessed 2024-12-01).

5 Freedom of expression as more than an individual right

This section contains an overview over the most important legal instruments and public policies on freedom of expression on UN and EU level and, in addition, some examples from the national level.

Freedom of expression is considered a fundamental aspect of democracy and highly respected in most democracies over the world (cf. Chapter 2). The principle is enshrined in international legal instruments on, for example, UN and EU level as well as in national legal instruments. Freedom of expression as an international legal principle was established in the Universal Declaration on Human Rights (UDHR) in the middle of the 20th century. The principle has however existed as highly valued long before and justified in various theories of free speech. Constitutional protection is, with some exceptions, of later date. Sweden (at that time including Finland) was the first country adopting a constitutional act on freedom of expression (or rather freedom of press) already in the middle of the 18th century (Carlsson & Goldberg 2017; Nokkala 2017). The meaning and the scope of freedom of expression is unsurprisingly not diverse.

The justifications of freedom of expression presented in Chapter 2 should be kept in mind when interpreting the legal instruments. We will give some examples of the most important legal instruments and how they have been interpreted. In Chapter 7 we will come back to the theories justifying freedom of expression when analysing how online anti-gender hate speech are handled.

5.1 The right to and the responsibility of freedom of expression

UDHR states in Article 19:

> Everyone has the right to freedom of opinion and expression; this right includes freedom to hold opinions without interference and to seek, receive and impart information and ideas through any media and regardless of frontiers.

DOI: 10.4324/9781003383062-5

The International Covenant on Civil and Political Rights (ICCPR) expresses the freedom of expression in a similar way, also in Article 19:

> 2. Everyone shall have the right to freedom of expression; this right shall include freedom to seek, receive and impart information and ideas of all kinds, regardless of frontiers, either orally, in writing or in print, in the form of art, or through any other media of his choice.

As the UDHR, the article in ICCPR also expresses that everyone shall have the right to hold opinions without interference, in the first clause of the same article.

The European Convention on Human Rights (ECHR) expresses the freedom slightly different, but its meaning is the same. Art. 10, 1st clause in ECHR states that everyone's '*right* to freedom of expression including freedom to hold opinions and to receive and impart information and ideas' is declared. And also, the principle of *non-censorship* expressed as '*without interference by public authority* and regardless of frontiers'.

Neither UDHR nor ICCPR explicitly points out the subject which may not interfere with the right. ECHR on the contrary does; the freedom for 'everyone' may not be interfered with by public authorities. This is predominantly how the right is perceived, namely as an individual right that should be protected from state restraints, or censorship. However, all three legal instruments open for restraints in some specific situations. UDHR in the second section of Article 29 states:

> In the exercise of his rights and freedoms, everyone shall be subject only to such limitations as are determined by law solely for the purpose of securing due recognition and respect for the rights and freedoms of others and of meeting the just requirements of morality, public order and the general welfare in a democratic society.

And, the third section of Article 19 of the ICCPR states:

> The exercise of the rights provided for in paragraph 2 of this article carries with it special duties and responsibilities. It may therefore be subject to certain restrictions, but these shall only be such as are provided by law and are necessary:
>
> (a) For respect of the rights or reputations of others;
> (b) For the protection of national security or of public order (ordre public), or of public health or morals.

And, according to ECHR article 10, section 2:

> The exercise of these freedoms carries with it duties and responsibilities, and may be subject to such formalities, conditions, restrictions or penalties as are prescribed by law and are necessary in a democratic society, in the interests of national security, territorial integrity or public safety, for the prevention of disorder or crime, for the protection of health or morals, for the protection of the reputation or rights of others, for preventing the disclosure of information received in confidence, or for maintaining the authority and impartiality of the judiciary.

The right to freedom of expression is *not* an unrestricted right to act as one pleases; it carries inherent duties and responsibilities. Balancing these rights requires both self-reflection and respect for others. An example showing the need for balancing the importance of being respectful and the reluctance towards restrictions in law, is the following statement by the UN High Commissioner for Human Rights Volker Türk in June 2023. He called on everyone to work together to build a more respectful and civil world, and for effective action to end hate speech, ahead of the International Day for Countering Hate Speech on 18 June. 'Rather than criminalizing protected speech, we need States and companies to take urgent steps to address incitement to hatred and violence' (UN Human Rights Chief 2023). What could also be noted here is that not only the States but also the companies are expected to take responsibility.

Even though the right to freedom of expression as a starting point protects all sorts of expressions, also those that offend, shock or disturb the State or any sector of the population, the right is not absolute. It might and should be proportionately balanced against other legitimate aims, provided by law. Such legitimate aims are, according to Art. 29 UDHR, 'securing due recognition and respect for the rights and freedoms of others and of meeting the just requirements of morality, public order and the general welfare in a democratic society'. Art. 19 ICCPR states similar aims: 'respect of the rights or reputations of others' and 'the protection of national security or of public order (ordre public), or of public health or morals'. Furthermore, ECHR Art. 10 points out:

> Conditions, restrictions or penalties as are prescribed by law and are necessary in a democratic society, in the interests of national security, territorial integrity or public safety, for the prevention of disorder or crime, for the protection of health or morals, for the protection of the reputation or rights of others, for preventing the disclosure of information received in confidence, or for maintaining the authority and impartiality of the judiciary.

The restrictions must always be proportionate, as concluded in *Handyside v. United Kingdom*, p. 49, para. 2:

> Subject to paragraph 2 of Article 10 (art. 10-2), it is applicable not only to 'information' or 'ideas' that are favourably received or regarded as inoffensive or as a matter of indifference, but also to those that offend, shock or disturb the State or any sector of the population. Such are the demands of that pluralism, tolerance and broadmindedness without which there is no 'democratic society'. This means, amongst other things, that every 'formality', 'condition', 'restriction' or 'penalty' imposed in this sphere must be proportionate to the legitimate aim pursued.

And the Special Rapporteur on violence against women, its causes and consequences, declares that 'freedom of expression is not, however, an absolute right, given that it cannot be invoked to justify language or other forms of expression designed to incite discrimination, hostility or violence (International Covenant on Civil and Political Rights, art. 20 (2)), including online violence against women' (A/HRC/38/47, para. 52).

If the balancing results in an advantageous for other interests than the individual right to freedom of expression, it is often perceived as a 'restriction' of the right. For example, criminalisation of hate speech is perceived as a restriction and something that should be avoided in order to protect freedom of expression. The difficulties in balancing basic principles are stressed by the Special Rapporteur:

> Online gender-based abuse and violence assaulted the basic principles of equality under international law and freedom of expression and underlined that ensuring an Internet free from gender-based violence enhanced women's empowerment. They also highlighted the fact that women victims and survivors needed transparent and fast responses and effective remedies, which could only be achieved if both States and private actors worked together and exercised due diligence to eliminate online violence against women.
>
> (A/HRC/38/47, para. 52)

However, if some individuals and groups are free to express offensive meanings with the consequences that other individual and groups are silenced, a laissez-faire attitude may in fact lead to a restriction of freedom of expression on a societal level. On the contrary, an active attitude to promote everyone's freedom of expression by emphasising everyone's responsibility to be respectful and not hateful can be seen as a strengthening of the *common good* even though some stakeholders are asked to be more respectful in their expressions and might see it as they are restricted.

5.2 The democratic rationale

The democratic rationale for freedom of expression mentioned above (Kenyon, Svensson & Edström 2017) is said to be the most frequently considered rationale within law (Barendt 2005, 20), and in Sweden it has impregnated the extensive and detailed legal regulation on freedom of expression for many years (Axberger 1984, 21; Bull 2006, 334).

> Beyond longevity – the Freedom of the Press Act dates from 1766 – noteworthy elements include: the degree to which the approach differentiates between media and non-media speech; strong protection provided to media sources; rights of access to information held by public authorities; special procedural protections for mediated speech, which in practice mean courts have only a minor role in determining the limits of speech; and the level of detail about speech in the constitutional Acts themselves.
>
> (Kenyon, Svensson & Edström 2017)

The role of the state has been to support the environment for speech, and this role is anchored in both constitutional acts and in statutes regulating, for example, the media and public service (Kenyon 2014, 2016; Karppinen 2016). The purpose of freedom of expression is expressed in three constitutional acts. According to *Tryckfrihetsförordningen* (TF – the Freedom of the Press Act) with its scope on printed media it is 'to secure the free exchange of opinion and availability of comprehensive information', information 'from all sides', and, according to the Free act *Yttrandefrihetsgrundlagen* (YGL – Fundamental Law on Freedom of Expression) covering broadcasting and other media than printed, the purpose is expressed similarly as 'to secure the free exchange of opinion, free and comprehensive information, and freedom of artistic creation'.

The state's enabling function for democratic free speech is thus highlighted explicitly in Sweden, where state policy has a role in promoting and deepening democracy through safeguarding free speech (SOU 1975: 79, p. 126; SOU 1995: 37, p. 156) and to create prerequisites for plurality (Dir. 2015: 26, p. 2). However, rhetoric about this aspect of free speech may be changing. For example, a 2015 official government report on media policy (SOU 2015: 94, p. 37) describes the state's relationship to free speech in ambiguous terms. It suggests: 'Every aspect of state governance can … be interpreted as infringements of these fundamental freedoms' of speech and information, but it also reaffirms the state's purpose in media policy is 'to create as free a society as possible where diversity of media can secure the rights and interests of all citizens'.

Despite the emphasis on the State's role in actively promoting freedom of expression within a participatory democracy model (see Chapter 2), there remains a notable hesitation to implement measures countering anti-gender hate speech. This hesitation is striking. Online hate speech (*näthat*), while not a legal concept, is addressed through various legal provision that focus exclusively on hate speech based on ethnicity and sexual orientation (Antigona Research Group 2020). Sex/gender, however, is notably absent.

5.3 Balancing freedom of expression and gender equality

Anti-gender hate speech, often discriminatory against women through gender stereotypes or acts of violence, has increasingly been recognised by UN and European/EU bodies as a legitimate basis for balancing freedom of expression. However, this perspective is not fully reflected, not even in the Swedish context. Despite its reputation as one of the most gender-equal countries in the world (Hellum et al. 2024; Svensson 2001), Sweden has not been a forerunner in this area. When balancing gender equality and freedom of expression, the latter appears to be given greater weight (Svensson & Edström 2014; Edström 2017).

In Italy the principle of freedom of expression, enshrined in the Constitution by article n°21[1] and constituting a pillar of the Italian legal system, should be balanced with respect for essential other legally protected interests, in particular respect for human dignity. In regard to this balance, expressive language should necessarily be limited when it exceeds and breaks the social and juridical aims for the recognition of this freedom. In this context, the phenomenon of hate speech is included.

One of the first specific provisions in this respect is the Constitutional Law n°645 (20th June 1952; the so-called Scelba Law), which forbids the reorganisation in any form of the banned fascist party, punishes the promotion of fascism, and the reintroduction of the typical practices of the former fascist party and regime.

The objective of this law was to penalise the phenomena of discrimination and protest by fascist movements in the immediate aftermath of the second world war, which were contrary to constitutional principles (Nocera 2018).

However, nowadays the temporary Commission for fighting the phenomena of intolerance, racism, antisemitism, and incitement to hatred and violence, established during the 18th legislature and attached to the Italian Senate, considers that there is a mismatch between the law and the social reality. In fact, in order to take action against the crimes envisaged by the 'Scelba Law', this Commission reiterated that it is necessary to demonstrate the subjective willingness of alleged perpetrators, which is very difficult to prove given that, for example, it is not enough if the subject simply says an explicit sentence, but it is also necessary to prove the real willingness to reconstitute the fascist party (Commissione straordinaria per il contrasto dei fenomeni di intolleranza, razzismo, antisemitismo e istigazione all'odio e alla violenza 2022).

Spain recognises freedom of speech as a fundamental human right under Article 20 of the Spanish Constitution. This right is directly applicable, with its only limits being other fundamental rights, particularly the rights to honour, privacy, and personal image. There is no specific law guaranteeing this right; instead, abuses involving attacks on honour, privacy, or personal image are addressed through civil jurisdiction.

The legal response to anti-gender hate speech varies depending on the jurisdiction in Spain. When such speech meets the criteria to be classified as a crime, it falls under criminal jurisdiction. However, when it is considered a violation of honour, privacy, or personal image, it is addressed in civil jurisdiction. This distinction has significant implications for victims: criminal procedures are free of charge, while civil procedures involve costs for legal representation. Additionally, if a civil claim is dismissed, the court may impose judicial costs on the applicant.

In recent years several statements of influential actors on *the global and European arenas* have supported that anti-gender hate speech hinders a diversity of voices and thus is an obstacle to achieve gender equality and a democratic problem. For instance, the UN Special Rapporteur on the promotion and protection of freedom of opinion and expression has declared; 'despite the impressive gains made by women, gender equality in freedom of expression remains a distant goal' (A/76/258). In the report, the special rapporteur examines the challenges that women face, offline and online, and analyses the relevant legal standards and the responsibilities of States and companies.

UN Women and the United Nations have highlighted a shadow pandemic in the form of digital violence and harassment in the footsteps of the Covid-19 pandemic (UN Women 2020). The theme for the International Women's day 2023 was how digital technic may be used to promote gender equality but also how it may be used to the opposite, how it creates new platforms for harassment and violence against women (International Women's Day 2023). Even though the freedom of expression was formulated in a time when digital technic was not invented the freedom today is exercised in the digital space with the use of ICT and the Internet, including the right to seek, receive and impart information freely on the Internet without censorship or other interference (A/HRC/38/47, para. 52).

In a report on online violence against women and girls from a human rights perspective by the Special Rapporteur on violence against women, its causes and consequences, the Rapporteur states that 'online and ICT-facilitated forms of violence against women have become increasingly common, particularly with the use, every day and everywhere, of social media platforms and other technical applications' (A/HRC/38/47, para. 12). The transformative potential of the international human rights instruments is confirmed in the report.

> Even though the core international human rights instruments, including those on women's rights, were drafted before the advent of ICT, they provide a global and dynamic set of rights and obligations with *transformative potential*, and have a key role to play in the *promotion and protection*

> of fundamental human rights, including a woman's rights to live *a life free from violence, to freedom of expression,* to privacy, to have access to information shared through ICT, and other rights.
>
> (A/HRC/38/47, para. 13)

States should ensure that their legal frameworks adequately protect all women's human rights online, including the right to life free from violence, freedom of expression and access to information, and the right to privacy and data protection (A/HRC/38/47, para. 95). Despite these obligations 'law enforcement bodies often trivialise online violence against women, and their actions are unfortunately often characterised by a victim-blaming attitude when dealing with these cases. The result of this attitude is a culture of silence and underreporting where women victims are reluctant to speak out for fear of being blamed' (A/HRC/38/47, para. 68). Also, the presence of 'online abuse against women journalists and women in the media are a direct attack on women's visibility and full participation in public life' (A/HRC/38/47, para. 29; see also OSCE 2016; CPJ 2016).

Women's silenced voices, a consequence of attacks from individuals or groups, is a problem that has started to gain attention on an international, regional and national political level. The UN Special Rapporteur Irene Khan declared in her *Report on the promotion and protection of the right to freedom of opinion and expression* (A/76/258) that the harm caused by online violence, sexist hate speech and disinformation may prevent women from being heard at all. And since online networks in the digital age today are the dominant space for communication, such silencing reduces diversity and affects the democratic debate. The Rapporteur continued to declare that the ability of women to make themselves heard is a key measure of democratic freedom, in addition to gender equality.

In another report, *Reinforcing media freedom and the safety of journalists in the digital age* (A/HRC/50/29), the same Special Rapporteur, Irene Khan, pointed at the fact that violent attacks on journalists with impunity, including online gender-based violence, legal harassment and targeted surveillance of journalists, censorship of content and manipulation of regulatory authorities have at times been entrenched, aggravated and augmented by digital technology. This is severe, according to the Rapporteur, given the importance of journalism as a public good, as a key pillar of democracy, and the societal relevance of independent, free and pluralistic news media.

The Council of Europe Group of Experts on Action against Violence against Women and Domestic Violence (GREVIO), which monitors the implementation of the Istanbul Convention has also increasingly focused its attention on online violence (Council of Europe n.d.). In its general recommendation in 2021 on the digital dimensions of violence (GREVIO General Recommendation no. 1), the group declared that online violence has severe implications on democratic participation, and in specific for women's participatory rights online. Participation is one of the central components in a democracy (V-dem), emphasised in western democracies, explicitly expressed by, for example, the Swedish government on the webpage explaining what is democracy (*Vad är demokrati?*).

In February 2024 the European Parliament reached a political agreement with the Council on the European Commission's proposal in 2022 for a directive on combating violence against women and domestic violence (Directive (EU) 2024/1385 of the European Parliament and of the Council of 14 May 2024 on combating violence against women and domestic violence). Reasons for the proposal, targeting such things as cyber-harassment and misogynous hate speech, were said to be that

> woman in general, more frequently experience cyber violence based on their sex or gender, in particular sexual forms of cyber violence. Women are systematically targeted online by violent right wing extremist groups and terrorist groups intending to spread hatred against them. The so-called 'incel' (involuntary celibate) movement, for instance, incites to violence against women online and promotes such violence as heroic acts. Cyber violence particularly impacts women active in public life, such as politicians, journalists and human rights defenders. This can have the effect of silencing women, hindering their societal participation and undermining the principle of democracy as enshrined in the Treaty on European Union.
>
> (COM[2022] 105 final 2022/0066 [COD], p. 2)

Moreover, the Commission has declared that 'hate speech and hate crime undermine the very foundations of a democratic and pluralistic society and the common values enshrined in Article 2 of the TEU' (COM[2022] 105 final 2022/0066 [COD], p. 8).

In addition, the challenge of hate speech has also been discussed, and the Commission has proposed to extend the list of EU crimes to include hate crimes and hate speech (including anti-gender hate speech), see COM/2021/777 and an in-depth discussion in Öberg (2024).

Anti-gender hate speech as a threat against democracy has also been addressed *in Sweden* in recent years. The accentuated threat against journalists, elected officials and artists has been met in the Swedish action plan 'To the Defence of the Free Word' (2017). Several proposals are presented to strengthen the protection of these groups, among them strengthened legal protection for journalists. In a Swedish Government Communication presenting a strategy against violent extremism and terrorism (Skr. 2023/24: 56) hate rhetoric is considered a threat against democracy followed by certain activities with the purpose of weakening democracy and hollowing out the trust for society and its institutions. Hate rhetoric increased during the pandemic (Skr. 2023/24: 56, 7). Access to digital media that can be used anonymously or under false identities has increased the possibility of exposing elected officials for, for example, online hate. Misogynic and other expressions and false news are considered as hurting democracy because such expressions might contribute to harassment and mobbing of groups that are underrepresented in the political life (SKR 2023). A research overview (CVE 2022) shows that misogyny is central to violent and extreme milieus, connected to a conservative understanding of gender. Men and women are essentially understood as different and are expected to have different roles in society. One way to express misogynic opinions is to argue for the reintroduction of male supremacy in public space. The violent extremist milieus are dominated by men and violence is used to claim male status.

The democracy aspect of certain voices being silenced is also emphasised in a Swedish government report on strengthened protection provided by criminal law for anti-gender hate crimes (not in specific hate speech; SOU 2023: 80, 382). A strengthened protection in criminal law sends a message not only to the perpetrator but also to society in general that certain crimes are seen very serious because they oppose to basic ideas in a democratic society such as equal treatment and protection against discrimination.

As mentioned above, freedom of expression includes both *non-censorship* and the need of *multiple and diverse voices*. This view of freedom of expression often means a special obligation for media to be a diverse forum for debate and – through that diversity and the relative absence of censorship – a mechanism for scrutinising the exercise of power. Such accountability is an important implication of the democratic rationale for free speech. Democratic forms of government are commonly said to be aimed at holding power to account, in part through mediated speech. Public speech is not just directed by those with power, it is not only subject to prevailing social powers but interrogates those with power (Kenyon, Svensson & Edström 2017).

Emphasising these aspects of freedom of expression takes it beyond a bare liberty against government action. Free speech includes obligations for a certain 'state of affairs' to be sought. Alexy and Rivers (2010) used the concept of a state of affairs in relation to broadcasting freedom (and other constitutional rights in Germany), and it appears useful to adopt here. Free speech involves not just what the state should refrain from doing, but also what the state and others should do to support the environment for speech (Kenyon 2014, 2016; Karppinen 2016). The changing and uncertain media environment may increase the challenges for state action to support diverse speech, but it does not remove the value of such efforts.

5.4 Concluding remarks

Freedom of expression is a fundamental aspect of democracy and as such a means to achieve democracy. The most important legal instruments and public policies on freedom of expression, when viewed through the lens of justification theories, reveal a more nuanced understanding of freedom of expression beyond an individual right. It is commonly valued for multiple reasons, an aid in discovering truth or developing knowledge, to serve people's interest in self-development or autonomy, and necessary for democratic forms of self-government. A democratic framing implies that freedom of expression has two equally important aspects, non-censorship and a diversity of voices. The most basic justification for freedom of expression is that it serves democracy, or the common good. This way of perceiving freedom of expression and the link between freedom of expression and democracy, is central to democracies. Sweden has a unique legal protection for a broad definition of freedom of expression. The state's enabling function for democratic free speech is essential. The role of state policy is to promote and deepen democracy through safeguarding free speech and to create prerequisites for plurality.

Note

1 Anyone has the right to freely express their thoughts in speech, writing or any other form of communication. The press may not be subjected to any authorisation or censorship. Seizure may be permitted only by judicial order stating the reason and only for offences expressly determined by the law on the press or in case of violation of the obligation to identify the persons responsible for such offences. In such cases, when there is absolute urgency and timely intervention of the judiciary is not possible, a periodical may be confiscated by the criminal police, which shall immediately and in no case later than 24 hours refer the matter to the judiciary for validation. In default of such validation in the following 24 hours, the measure shall be revoked and considered null and void. The law may introduce general provisions for the disclosure of financial sources of periodical publications. Publications, performances and other exhibits offensive to public morality shall be prohibited. Measures of preventive and repressive measure against such violations shall be established by law (Constitution of the Italian Republic).

References

Literature

Alexy, R. & Rivers, J. (2010), *A theory of constitutional rights*. Oxford University Press.

Antigona Research Group (2020), *Report on the state of the art on anti-gender hate speech*. https://cris.unibo.it/retrieve/e1dcb335-f518-7715-e053-1705fe0a6cc9/REPORT%20ON%20THE%20STATE%20OF%20THE%20ART%20ON%20ANTI%20GENDER%20HATE%20SPEECH.pdf.

Axberger, H.-G. (1984), *Tryckfrihetens gränser*. Liber Förlag.

Barendt, E. (2005), *Freedom of speech*, 2nd ed. Oxford University Press.

Bull, T. (2006), 'Appendix 8 to Part 2 of SOU 2006:96: Sverige. Tryck- och yttrandefrihetsberedningen,Ett nytt grundlagsskydd för tryck- och yttrandefriheten? Tryck- och yttrandefrihetsberedningen inbjudertill debatt: delbetänkande'. www.researchgate.net/publication/312053494_Building_and_Sustaining_Freedom_of_Expression_Considering_Sweden (accessed 2024-12-13).

Carlsson, U., Goldberg, D. & Nordicom (2017), *The legacy of Peter Forsskål: 250 years of freedom of expression*. Nordicom.

Center mot våldsbejakande extremism (CVE) (2022). https://cve.se/publikationer/manmaskulinitetochvaldsbejakandeextremismenkunskapsoversikt.5.11258e6a184d17a7b2ca1b.html.

Committee to Protect Journalists (CPJ) (2016), *Attacks on the press: Gender and media freedom worldwide*. Bloomberg.

Edström, M. (2017), 'Utan jämställdhet ingen yttrandefrihet'. In *Den Svære Ytringsfrihed – Nordiske Røster*. Nordic Council of Ministers.

Hellum, A., Ikdahl, I., Blaker Strand, V. & Svensson, E.-M. (2024), *Nordic equality and anti-discrimination laws in the throes of change: Legal developments in Sweden, Finland, Norway, and Iceland*. Taylor & Francis. https://doi.org/10.4324/9781003172840.

Karppinen, K. (2016), 'Beyond positive and negative conceptions of free speech'. In Edström, M., Kenyon, A. T. & Svensson, E.-M. (Eds.), *Blurring the lines. Market-driven and democracy-driven freedom of expression*. Nordicom.

Kenyon, A. T. (2014), 'Assuming free speech', *Modern Law Review*, 77(3), 379–408. https://doi.org/10.1111/1468-2230.12071.

Kenyon, A. T. (2016), 'Who, what, why and how. Questions for positive free speech and media systems'. In Edström, M., Kenyon, A. T. & Svensson, E.-M. (Eds.), *Blurring the lines: Market-driven and democracy-driven freedom of expression*. Nordicom.

Kenyon, A. T., Svensson, E.-M. & Edström, M. (2017), 'Building and sustaining freedom of expression: Considering Sweden', *Nordicom Review*, 38(1), 31–45. https://doi.org/10.1515/nor-2016-0043.

Nocera, A. (2018), 'Manifestazioni fasciste e apologia del fascismo tra attualità e nuove prospettive incriminatrici', *Diritto Penale Contemporaneo*. https://archiviodpc.dirittopenaleuomo.org/upload/7915-nocera2018a.pdf.

Nokkala, E. (2017), 'World's first freedom of writing and of the press ordinance as history of political thought'. In Carlsson, U. & Goldberg, D. (Eds.), *The legacy of Peter Forsskål: 250 years of freedom of expression*. Nordicom.

Öberg, J. (2024), *The normative foundations for EU criminal justice. Powers, limits and justifications*. Hart.

Svensson, E.-M. (2001), 'Sex equality: Changes in politics, jurisprudence and feminist legal studies'. In Nousiainen, K., Gunnarsson, Å., Lundström, K. & Niemi-Kiesiläinen, J. (Eds.), *Responsible selves, women in the Nordic legal culture*. Ashgate.

Svensson, E.-M. & Edström, M. (2014), 'Freedom of expression vs. gender equality: Conflicting values when regulating gender stereotypes in advertising', *Tidsskrift for Rettsvitenskap*, 127(5), 479–511.

Court cases

European Court of Human Rights

Handyside v. United Kingdom, appl. No 5493/72, 7.12. 1976.

Public documents and laws

International (UN)

A/76/258 (2021), *Promotion and protection of the right to freedom of opinion and expression*. United Nations General Assembly. Note by the Secretary-General. https://documents.un.org/doc/undoc/gen/n21/212/16/pdf/n2121216.pdf (accessed 2024-10-23).

A/HRC/38/47 (2018), *Report of the Special Rapporteur on violence against women, its causes and consequences on online violence against women and girls from a human rights perspective.* United Nations General Assembly. Note by the Secretariat. https://documents-dds-ny.un.org/doc/UNDOC/GEN/G18/184/58/PDF/G1818458.pdf?OpenElement (accessed 2024-10-23).

A/HRC/50/29 (2022), *Reinforcing media freedom and the safety of journalists in the digital age.* Report of the Special Rapporteur on the promotion and protection of the right to freedom of opinion and expression. United Nations General Assembly https://documents.un.org/doc/undoc/gen/g22/323/44/pdf/g2232344.pdf (accessed 2024-10-23).

International Covenant on Civil and Political Rights (ICCPR), New York, 16 Dec. 1966, entered into force 23 Mar. 1976, the provisions of article 41, entered into force 28 Mar. 1979. Human Rights Committee. www.ohchr.org/sites/default/files/ccpr.pdf (accessed 2024-10-23).

International Women's Day (2023), www.unwomen.org/en/news-stories/in-focus/2023/03/in-focus-international-womens-day (accessed 2024-10-23).

UN Human Rights Chief (16 June 2023), 'Hate speech has no place in our world'. www.ohchr.org/en/press-releases/2023/06/un-human-rights-chief-hate-speech-has-no-place-our-world (accessed 2024-10-23).

UN Women (2020) The Shadow Pandemic: Violence against women during COVID-19. www.unwomen.org/en/news/in-focus/in-focus-gender-equality-in-covid-19-response/violence-against-women-during-covid-19 (accessed 2025-02-24).

Universal Declaration of Human Rights (UDHR) (10 Dec. 1948), U.N.G.A. Res. 217 A (III) (1948). www.ohchr.org/en/human-rights/universal-declaration/translations/english (accessed 2024-10-23).

International (Council of Europe and EU)

Council of Europe (n.d.), 'Cyberviolence against women'. www.coe.int/en/web/cyberviolence/cyberviolence-against-women, https://digitallibrary.un.org/record/1641160/files/A_HRC_38_47-EN.pdf (accessed 2024-10-23).

Directive (EU) 2024/1385 of the European Parliament and of the Council of 14 May 2024 on combating violence against women and domestic violence. https://eur-lex.europa.eu/legal-content/EN/TXT/?uri=OJ%3AL_202401385 (accessed 2024-10-23).

European Commission (2021), COM(2021) 777 final communication from the Commission to the European Parliament and the Council. *A more inclusive and protective Europe: Extending the list of EU crimes to hate speech and hate crime.* https://eur-lex.europa.eu/legal-content/EN/TXT/?uri=CELEX:52021DC0777 (accessed 2024-12-01).

European Commission (2022), COM(2022) 105 final 2022/0066 (COD). *Proposal for a directive of the European Parliament and of the Council on combating violence against women and domestic violence.* https://eur-lex.europa.eu/legal-content/EN/TXT/PDF/?uri=CELEX:52022PC0105 (accessed 2024-10-23).

European Convention on Human Rights (ECHR). www.echr.coe.int/documents/convention_eng.pdf (accessed 2024-10-23).

Group of Experts on Action against Violence against Women and Domestic Violence (GREVIO), *General Recommendation no. 1 on the digital dimension of violence against women adopted on 20 October 2021.* https://rm.coe.int/grevio-rec-no-on-digital-violence-against-women/1680a49147 (accessed 2024-10-23).

Organization for Security and Co-operation in Europe (OSCE) (2016), *New challenges to freedom of expression: Countering online abuse of female journalists.* www.osce.org/files/f/documents/c/3/220411.pdf (accessed 2024-10-23).

Sweden

Dir. 2015: 26, *En mediepolitik för framtiden.* Kulturdepartementet. www.regeringen.se/contentassets/37c5138b3218403f8c31bbf1658c4e48/en-mediepolitik-for-framtiden-dir.-201526 (accessed 2024-10-24).

SKR (2023), *Rapport från Europarådets kommun- och regionskongress 2022, Hatretorik och falska nyheter.*

Skr. 2023/24: 56, *Nationell strategi mot våldsbejakande extremism och terrorism – förebygga, förhindra, skydda och hantera.* www.regeringen.se/contentassets/e30421686167432d87cfb77fbe2a6dad/nationell-strategi-mot-valdsbejakande-extremism-och-terrorism--forebygga-forhindra-skydda-och-hantera-skr-20232456/ (accessed 2024-11-27).

SOU 1975: 79, *Svensk Press. Statlig presspolitik.* Betänkande av 1972 års pressutredning. Göteborgs Offsettryckeri AB . https://filedn.com/ljdBas5OJsrLJOq6KhtBYC4/forarbeten/sou/1975/sou-1975-79.pdf (accessed 2024-11-27).

SOU 1995: 37, *Vårt dagliga blad – stöd till svensk dagspress.* Betänkande av Pressutredningen -94. Fritzes, Offentliga Publikationer. https://lagen.nu/sou/1995:37?attachment=index.pdf&repo=soukb&dir=downloaded (accessed 2024-11-27).

SOU 2015: 94, *Medieborgarna & medierna. En digital värld av rättigheter, skyldigheter – möjligheter och ansvar.* Delbetänkande av Medieutredningen, Elanders Sverige AB. www.regeringen.se/contentassets/aca20d317683426797fc15c0056004f3/medieborgarna--medierna.-en-digital-varld-av-rattigheter-skyldigheter--mojligheter-och-ansvar-sou-201594 (accessed 2024-11-27).

SOU 2023: 80, *Ett starkare straffrättsligt skydd – mot sexuella kränkningar, bedrägerier i vissa fall och brott med hatmotiv avseende kön.* Betänkande av Utredningen om barns skydd mot sexuella kränkningar samt vissa frågor om brott mot kvinnor och äldre. Elanders Sverige AB. www.regeringen.se/contentassets/e8ccf3b8d03c46db856bc850e8c453dc/ett-starkare-straffrattsligt-skydd--mot-sexuella-krankningar-bedragerier-i-vissa-fall-och-brott-med-hatmotiv-avseende-kon.-sou-202380 (accessed 2024-11-27).

To the Defence of the Free Word (2017), *Till det fria ordets försvar. Åtgärder mot utsatthet för hot och hat bland journalister, förtroendevalda och konstnärer, Regeringskansliet Kulturdepartementet.* www.regeringen.se/contentassets/b12e82d597d04444a11f2c227b7cc8c3/till-det-fria-ordets-forsvar.pdf (accessed 2024-10-24).

Vad är demokrati? (2023). www.riksdagen.se/sv/sa-fungerar-riksdagen/demokrati/vad-ar-demokrati (accessed 2024-10-24).

Other sources

Commissione straordinaria per il contrasto dei fenomeni di intolleranza, razzismo, antisemitismo e istigazione all'odio e alla violenza (2022), *Report a conclusione dell'indagine conoscitiva su natura, cause e sviluppi recenti del fenomeno dei discorsi d'odio, con particolare attenzione all'evoluzione della normativa europea in materia*. Senato della Repubblica Italiana. www.senato.it/service/PDF/PDFServer/DF/410798.pdf (accessed 2024-11-28).

Constitution of the Italian Republic, Senato della Repubblica. www.senato.it/documenti/repository/istituzione/costituzione_inglese.pdf (accessed 2024-12-01).

6 Combating anti-gender hate speech with criminal regulation

Online gender-based hate speech takes place in everyday life all over the globe. The ways and means to communicate online are constantly changing and are taking place 24/7 (UNESCO & UN Broadband Commission 2013; UN Women 2020). The expressions may take different shapes and cause different kinds of harm or public wrong, some parts that could fall outside the scope of criminal liability and some that should be included. Previous research has shown that the criminal legal system is fragmented and not up-to-date (Bladini 2020; McGlynn 2023). The criminal law system is inherently inert, which makes it ill-equipped to keep pace with the rapidly evolving forms of online harassment and is therefore not yet fully capable of addressing all such behaviours (www.genha.eu). In addition, not all expressions online are included in the constitutionally protected freedom of expression, as statements made in constitutionally protected media enjoy stronger legal safeguards compared to those made in non-protected platforms (Antigona Group 2020). In Chapter 5, we demonstrated the robust protection afforded to expressions in constitutionally protected media. Here, we will highlight the distinction between these and other types of expressions, with particular emphasis on the strong legal safeguards in Sweden. An example will illustrate the difference in the Swedish legal system:

> A well-known columnist, media personality, actor, and artist became one of the leading figures in the Swedish #MeToo movement during the autumn of 2017. Just a few days after The New York Times published the accusations against a renowned American film producer, she followed suit by accusing a well-established journalist of rape, adding the hashtag #MeToo in her social media post. The post, along with others, was picked up by the news and widely circulated. A few months later, she was reported to the police, prosecuted, and eventually convicted for gross defamation (Ganetz Hansson & Sveningsson 2022). During the criminal proceedings, she wrote a book about the alleged rape, other sexual offences, and the case in which she was convicted of gross defamation. The book was published through her own publishing company after her initial

DOI: 10.4324/9781003383062-6

publisher withdrew at a late stage, reportedly out of concern about potential lawsuits for gross defamation (Wikipedia, latest updated 2024). As the book was published at a publishing house, its content was protected under the Swedish constitutional Freedom of the Press Act. This act provides broader legal protections compared to content published on social media platforms. Under this legislation, a case concerning alleged crimes can only be initiated by the Chancellor of Justice, and the court is composed not only of a judge but also of a jury – a special formation of the Swedish judicial system reserved exclusively for cases under the Freedom of the Press Act). Just as the original publishing house had feared, the Chancellor of Justice prosecuted the author for gross defamation under the provisions in this act. The second trial concluded in March 2022, with the author being acquitted.

These two cases illustrate the robust protection provided under Sweden's constitutional acts compared to ordinary criminal legislation. This chapter contains an overview of ordinary criminal legislation and concludes with an examination of constitutional legislation.

The practical challenge of addressing anti-gender hate speech can be tackled through various means, of which criminal law being one of them. In schools and other societal institutions, states often use education to promote awareness about appropriate communication, both on- and offline (e.g. the NoHate Movement). On social media platforms, self-regulatory mechanisms aim to prevent offensive and illegal content, though their implementation varies widely (Antigona Research Group 2021). For instance, Telegram, known for its minimal regulation and moderation policies, has faced significant legal actions against its founder and CEO (BBC 2024).

Criminal law is not only the most powerful tool available to states for addressing societal problems but also carries significant normative force, shaping societal values and behaviour. However, in line with the fundamental principle of criminalisation, *ultima ratio*, criminal law should only be employed as a last resort – a concept elaborated in greater detail in Chapter 2.

The remainder of this chapter examines criminal law at both the European and national levels. While international law under the UN framework will not be discussed – since it does not require states to criminalise specific behaviours but merely to take measures to address certain issues (as detailed in Chapters 4 and 5) – this section provides an overview of European laws and public policies. It includes a brief comparison of legal frameworks applicable to anti-gender hate speech, alongside national regulations in selected European countries, with Sweden, Italy, and Spain serving as the primary examples.

Traditionally, criminal law has been a national concern, regulated exclusively at the domestic level. In recent years, however, European regulation has increasingly shaped the area of criminalisation, adding a supranational dimension to what was once a purely national domain.

6.1 Regulations and policies within European Union

In 2009, the Treaty of Lisbon came into effect, integrating judicial cooperation in criminal matters fully into the framework of EU law and policies, moving away from the previous model of intergovernmental cooperation.

The definition of hate speech can, as discussed in Chapter 2, vary across different contexts. The Council of Europe uses the definition in ECRI Recommendation No. 15, which is also the starting point for this book, see Chapter 1.[1] Hence, in accordance with that definition, we define hate speech as any form of denigration, hatred, or vilification directed at an individual or group, as well as any form of harassment, insult, negative stereotyping, stigmatisation, or threat towards such individuals or groups. This also includes the justification of these forms of expression based on 'race, colour, descent, national or ethnic origin, age, disability, language, religion or belief, sex, gender, gender identity, sexual orientation, or other personal characteristics or status'. The definition hence allows for a broad inclusion of various forms and types of actions that may constitute anti-gender hate speech, not all of which fall under the criminalised area in national jurisdictions. It should also be noted that hate speech is not a particular legal concept in all jurisdictions, for example, in Sweden.

Prior to the Istanbul Convention on preventing and combating violence against women and domestic violence, discussed in Chapter 4, the Council of Europe focused on equal treatment and combating discrimination (Council Directive 2000/43/EC) and cyber hate speech through criminalisation (AP to the Convention on Cybercrime) due to xenophobic and racist motives, but did not include gender.[2]

In this section, we examine legislation and policies both in terms of the actions covered by current regulations and those that fall outside the scope of the law. The purpose of this discussion is to establish a reference point, allowing us to illustrate not only what is regulated but also give examples of what remain unregulated within the framework of criminal law in this area. It is important to note that the concept of anti-gender hate speech used in this chapter is broader than the one applied in the rest of the book. Here, we align with the GENHA definition, which includes attacks based on sex, gender, sexual orientation, transgender identity, and transgender expressions. This broader definition helps us evaluate the extent of the existing regulations and highlights the gaps in criminal regulation related to anti-gender hate speech.

The European Parliament has advocated for stronger measures against gender-based violence. In 2014, it called for gender-based violence to be added to the list of serious crimes in Art. 83(1) of the TFEU, to establish a stronger legal basis for an EU directive with common definitions and minimum sanctions. The present list of EU crimes includes gender-based violence in a few forms: trafficking in human beings and sexual exploitation of women and children. Article 83 of the Treaty of Lisbon regulates the competence to establish 'minimum rules concerning the definition of criminal offences and sanctions in the areas of particularly serious crime with a cross-border dimension'. In 2021, the European Parliament adopted a new resolution recommending that gender-based violence be added to this list, which would harmonise cross-border protections and improve efforts to combat it.

The European Parliament proposed a directive to prevent and combat gender-based violence both online and offline, with a victim-centred approach aligned with the standards of the Istanbul Convention. This resolution preceded the European Commission's December 2021 proposal to add hate crime and hate speech to the EU's crime list, which would include certain forms of gender-based violence. The European Commission, with its March 2022 proposal, indicated that these initiatives would largely fulfil Parliament's objectives. In July 2022, the European Economic and Social Committee also supported adding violence against women to the list of EU crimes (Björk & Riba Giner 2024). The proposal from the European Parliament to add these crimes to the list of EU crimes was in the end rejected, as it needed a unanimous decision. Hence, the proposal was rebooted by the European Commission in 2023, proposed as new legislation on combating violence against women and domestic violence which was adopted on 7 May 2024 (Directive (EU) 2024/1385, mentioned in Chapters 1 and 4). The EU now has the first ever law to effectively fight violence against women and domestic violence. The Directive criminalises at EU level certain forms of violence against women offline and online and requires Member States to put in place robust measures of prevention, protection, access to justice, support, coordination and cooperation between authorities. The proposal's legal framework implies that violence against women should be included under the categories 'sexual exploitation of women and children and computer crime', to find legal basis in Art. 83(1) TFEU (cf. Öberg 2024).

Based on the Commission's proposal adopted on 8 March 2022, the Council adopted the EU Directive on combating violence against women and domestic violence (Directive (EU) 2024/1385 of the European Parliament and of the Council of 14 May 2024 on combating violence against women and domestic violence) on 7 May 2024, after the European Parliament approved the text on 24 April. Member States will have until 14 June 2027 to transpose the Directive into their national law and policy. The Directive criminalises at EU level certain forms of violence against women offline (female genital mutilation and forced marriage) and online (this may include some forms of non-consensual sharing of intimate images, cyber stalking, cyber harassment and incitement to hatred and violence on the ground of gender). It also provides targeted measures of protection, support, and access to justice for victims of any form of violence against women and domestic violence, where such acts are criminalised under national or EU law. Finally, it requires Member States to set up preventive measures, including specific measures to prevent rape and to promote the central role of consent in sexual relationships. It is noteworthy that the final version of the directive does not criminalise rape, despite initial support for this measure from the Commission, Parliament, and several Member States.

This directive on gender-based violence represents a significant step in combating violence against women and domestic violence, with a particular emphasis on cyberviolence. The directive builds on the EU's commitment to protecting fundamental rights, such as the right to non-discrimination, and seeks to harmonise relevant laws across the EU. It aims to complement the Istanbul Convention by strengthening protections against crimes like virtual pornography, which the Convention does not cover. While the proposal includes innovative aspects, such as addressing deepfake pornography, it also presents legal challenges, particularly regarding legal bases and the harmonisation of criminal law across the EU (Belloni 2024).

The Digital Services Act (DSA), adopted by EU in 2022, aims to make the online space safer. The regulation imposes various duties related to content moderation on social media platforms and came into force in February 2024. It offers multiple safeguards for users' free speech rights against platform actions (this is about strengthening the freedom of expression by means of regulating what is allowed to express). It mandates that platforms provide clear information regarding content restrictions within their terms of service and ensures that these restrictions are applied and enforced with due consideration for users' free speech rights (Article 14). Additionally, platforms are required to furnish a statement of reasons to users whose content has been restricted or whose accounts have been suspended or terminated (Article 17). Moreover, platforms must establish an internal complaint-handling system, allowing users to challenge decisions that limit their content or accounts (Article 20).

The three primary objectives of the DSA are (1) to ensure transparency in the operation of platforms, (2) to safeguard the enforcement of fundamental rights on online and social media, and (3) to guarantee legal recourse for individuals against decisions made by platforms.

The European Commission decided to open infringement proceedings by sending a letter of formal notice to Spain and Sweden, among other member states, as either they had not designated the competent authorities - the so-called Digital Services Coordinators - to implement the Digital Services Act, or they had not empowered these authorities to carry out the tasks required by the Act, or both. The Member States had until 17 February 2024 to designate these authorities. Digital Services Coordinators supervise online intermediaries (such as online platforms) established in their territories and serve as the first point of contact for individuals and businesses seeking to resolve complaints related to those services (European Commission n.d.).

In 2020, the Council of Europe established a Committee of Experts on Combating Hate Speech with the mandate to draft recommendations for addressing and regulating hate speech within the framework of human rights (Council of Europe n.d.). This initiative reflects the growing need for comprehensive strategies to tackle hate speech, including its manifestations in digital spaces.[3] The Committee's work culminated in the adoption of the Recommendation of the Committee of Ministers to Member States on Combating Hate Speech (CM/Rec(2022)16) in May 20, 2022. This document is now a cornerstone in the effort to address hate speech, offering a comprehensive strategy that explicitly includes measures targeting its online dimension.

The Parliamentary Assembly of the Council of Europe has played a significant role in addressing online hate, notably through its 2144 (2017) Resolution 'Ending Cyberdiscrimination and Online Hate'. This resolution emphasises that hate speech extends beyond racism and xenophobia, encompassing other forms such as sexism. It asserts that behaviours deemed unacceptable offline should equally be condemned online, stating: 'Just like the face-to-face world, the internet must provide space to be critical, without providing space for hate speech, including incitement to violence' (PACE Resolution 2144, para. 2).[4] Despite much efforts over time, there remains a persistent reluctance to fully recognise sexist discourse as a form of hate speech. This hesitation continues to hinder a comprehensive approach to addressing gender-based hate in both offline and online spaces (Lillian 2017).

6.2 Criminal offences in a national context

This section explores how gender-based violence is addressed under criminal law in Sweden, Italy, and Spain. It examines both constitutional provisions and ordinary legal regulations, with a particular focus on the Swedish context.

6.2.1 Sweden

This section explores the Swedish legal regulation of hate crimes and hate speech, beginning with an introduction to the development of these concepts within legal discourse. It provides context for the regulatory framework and examines offences involving aggravated circumstances due to hate motives, as well as crimes regulated under constitutional acts. The review includes an analysis of the current legal framework and considers potential extensions to cover anti-gender hate speech and hate crimes. It also highlights areas that currently fall outside the scope of these regulations in Sweden, drawing on draft laws, legislative proposals, and relevant case law to provide additional insights. In addition, the section addresses the issue of criminal responsibility, focusing not only individual offenders but also other liable subjects. This includes individuals responsible for moderating electronic bulletin boards – such as social media platforms or specific sections within them – as well as publishers in media-related contexts. Finally, there is an ending section on policies and legal proposals.

6.2.1.1 Hate crime and hate speech: Relevant offences

The concept of hate crime was introduced into Swedish scholarly discourse in 1999 (Tiby 1999), having originated from the United States where it had already been in use for some time (Granström, Mellby & Tiby 2016, 11). In Swedish legislation, while there is no legal definition of either *hate crime* or *hate speech*, these terms are widely used legal, political, and public discourse. Instead of having a statutory definition, *hate crime* is often treated as a broad, overarching concept. Several Swedish authorities --including the Swedish National Council for Crime Prevention, the National Police Council, and the Prosecution Authority --have adopted a working definition. According to these bodies, a hate crime is defined as:

> an offence directed towards a person, group, property, institution, or representative of these, motivated by fear, hostility, or hate against the offended on the grounds of race, color, national or ethnic origin, religious belief, sexual orientation, or gender identity or expression as perceived by the perpetrator.[5]

The definition emphasises that hate crimes are not only directed at individuals but may also target groups, property, or institutions. Central to this definition is the motivation behind the crime, which is driven by bias or prejudice related to the victim's identity, as perceived by the perpetrator.

Furthermore, while *hate speech* is not separately defined, it is often understood as a specific form of hate crime, focusing on expressions that incite hatred against particular groups or individuals based on similar grounds. Despite the absence of a statutory definition, the terms *hate crime* and *hate speech* are pervasive in legal, political, and public contexts in Sweden. This usage underscores their importance in addressing issues related to discrimination, prejudice, and societal harm. The Swedish legal regulation of the two will be discussed here, both as a review of the current legal situation and through examples of possible extensions of the legal regulation to cover anti-gender, sexist, and anti-feminist hate speech and hate crime. In addition, we will indicate what currently falls outside the legal scope of hate crime and hate speech in Sweden.

The criminal regulation of hate speech and hate crime operates on two levels: the first level, addresses specific offences, and the second introduces more severe punishments for crimes committed with a hate motive. The first level, the criminalisation of specific acts, is typically divided into two offences: *agitation against a population group*, regulated in Chapter 16, Section 8 of the *Brottsbalken* (BrB –Swedish Criminal Code, commonly referred to as hate speech), and *unlawful discrimination*, outlined in Chapter 16, Section 9.

A third offence may also be relevant in the context of online hate crime and hate speech: *conspiracy* to commit an offence may apply if an individual seeks to instigate another person to commit a crime.

The second level concerns aggravating circumstances, which result in harsher penalties for crimes motivated by hatred. This corresponds to the concept of hate crime and is regulated in Chapter 29, Section 2, Paragraph 7 BrB.

Additionally, another provision in BrB is relevant to the theme of hate speech and hate crime. This concerns the crime of *defamation*, found in Chapter 5, Section 1 (and gross defamation in Section 2). Defamation does not typically fall under public prosecution and instead requires private prosecution. However, Chapter 5, Section 5 provides an exception, allowing a prosecutor to initiate proceedings 'if this is considered to be called for in the public interest and the prosecution relates to … 3. Insulting behaviour by allusion to race, colour, national or ethnic origin, religious belief, sexual orientation, or transgender identity or expression'. While this provision relates more to legal procedure than to substantive criminalisation, it remains an important component of the legal framework addressing hate speech and hate crimes.

Agitation against a population group

Although the concept of hate crime was not introduced into the Swedish legal discourse until the late 1990's, the offence *agitation against a population group* has a longer history in Swedish criminal law, having been established in 1948 in the aftermath of the Second World War. Its original purpose was to address the increasing prevalence of anti-Semitic propaganda. The criminalisation encompassed offences targeting groups based on origin, descent, or religious belief. This new criminal regulation marked a restriction on the constitutional freedom of speech, with the aim of safeguarding public order and safety (SOU 1944: 69; prop. 1948: 80).

Over time, the protected groups were defined as race, colour, national or ethnic origin and religious belief. In 2003, the regulation expanded to include sexual orientation (prop. 2001/02: 59). The offence is codified in BrB as *agitation against a population group (Hets mot folkgrupp)* under Chapter 16, Section 8:

> A person who, in a statement or other communication that is disseminated, inciting violence, threatens or expresses contempt towards a population group, another such group of people or an individual belonging to any of these groups, by allusion to race, colour, national or ethnic origin, religious belief, sexual orientation or transgender identity or expression, is guilty of *agitation against a population group* and is sentenced to imprisonment for at most two years.
>
> …
>
> If the offence is gross, the person is guilty of gross agitation against a population group and is sentenced to imprisonment for at least six months and at most four years. When assessing whether the offence is

> gross, particular consideration is given to whether the communication had particularly threatening or offensive content and was disseminated to a large number of people in a way that was liable to attract considerable attention.
>
> (Act 2024: 340)

Older version (before 2018): Agitation against a national or ethnic group

> A person who, in a disseminated statement or communication, threatens or expresses contempt for a national, ethnic or other such group of persons with allusion to race, colour, national or ethnic origin or religious belief shall, be sentenced for *agitation against a national or ethnic group* to imprisonment for at most two years or, if the crime is petty, to a fine.
>
> (Law 1988: 835) (official translation) *(i.e. there was no protection against hate due to sexual orientation or transgender identity in the first version of 1988)*

The regulations indicate that, in the version from 1988, there was no legal protection for individuals targeted on the grounds of sexual orientation or transgender identity or expression. However, this was changed in 2003 to include sexual orientation (prop. 2001/02: 59), and in 2019, it was further expanded to include transgender identity and expression (prop 2017/18: 59).

In conclusion, current legislation includes protections based on sexual orientation, transgender identity and transgender expression. However, it lacks provisions addressing hate speech motivated by other forms of sexism. Notably, gender is not included under the criminal regulation of agitation against a population group, despite having been proposed and debated during previous amendments and expansions of the protected groups. Similarly, political beliefs, including those related to gender equality, are not covered by this regulation.[6]

Unlawful discrimination

Another criminal regulation that protects the same groups – namely individuals targeted on the grounds of race, colour, national or ethnic origin, religious belief, sexual orientation, or transgender identity or expression – is the offence of unlawful discrimination, regulated in BrB, Chapter 16, Section 9. This provision specifically addresses discriminatory actions carried out by business operators, their employees, or individuals organising public gatherings:

> A business operator who, in their business activities, discriminates against a person on grounds of race, colour, national or ethnic origin, religious belief, sexual orientation or transgender identity or expression by not assisting that person on the terms and conditions the operator applies to others in their business activities is guilty of *unlawful discrimination* and is sentenced to a fine or imprisonment for at most one year.

> The provisions of the first paragraph about a business operator also apply to anyone who is employed in business activities or otherwise acts on behalf of a business operator, and to anyone who is in public employment or holds elected office.
>
> An organiser of a public gathering or event, and anyone who is aids such an organiser, who discriminates against a person on grounds of race, colour, national or ethnic origin, religious belief, sexual orientation or transgender identity or expression by refusing them access to the gathering or event on the terms and conditions applied to others is also guilty of unlawful discrimination. (Act 2018: 540)

Although the regulation is part of the broader framework often associated with hate crimes, it differs in scope and application. Unlike regulations targeting online hate or harassment, unlawful discrimination primarily concerns business operators or organisers of public events and their responsibilities to treat individuals equally in the context of their activities. While hate motives and discrimination are relevant, the focus on commercial or public contexts places the offence somewhat outside the primary theme of online hate speech. Consequently, this regulation is mentioned here for completeness but is not discussed further in this review.

Conspiracy to commit an offence

Another possible offence in a similar context is conspiracy to commit an offence, particularly when one individual attempts to instigate another person to commit a crime. BrB, Chapter 23, Section 2, Paragraph 2:

> In cases specifically provided for, a person is guilty of conspiracy to commit an offence. 'Conspiracy' means that a person decides on the act in concert with another person, or that a person tries to instigate another person to commit it, or undertakes or offers to commit it.

This offence is particularly relevant to discussions on hate crimes when the motive qualifies as part of hate crime under Chapter 29, Section 2, Paragraph 7 of BrB, that will be further discussed below. Moreover, even when such actions do not fall under the scope of current legal definitions of hate crime, they may still constitute hate speech within a broader theoretical framework. For instance, if the act targets gender, sex, sexism, gender equality, or feminist ideas. This distinction highlights the discrepancy between actions that meet the theoretical criteria for hate speech or hate crimes and those that are formally recognised under existing legal definitions.

6.2.1.2 Regulation on hate motive as an aggravating circumstance

The regulation that explicitly identifies hate motives as an aggravating circumstance in sentencing was first proposed in a Government Bill in 1988 (Prop. 1987/88: 120) and further developed in 1993 (Prop. 1993/94: 101).

It was implemented in 1994, although courts already had the discretion to consider hate motives prior to the new regulation's formal adoption. This provision applies to crimes committed with a motive targeting a person or group based on race, skin colour, national or ethnic origin, religious beliefs, or similar circumstances (Prop. 1993/94: 101, p. 6).

In 2002, the regulation was amended to include sexual orientation as a ground for hate motives. This change mirrored the updates to the provisions on agitation against a population group. During the legislative process, the inclusion of transsexualism under the scope of sexual orientation was debated. However, the decision was made to limit the concept of sexual orientation to heterosexuality, homosexuality and bisexuality at the time. The rationale cited was the need for further knowledge and understanding of transgender identity and transgender expressions.

In 2019, the regulation was updated again to explicitly include transgender identity and transgender expression as grounds for hate motives. This addition marked a significant progress in acknowledging and addressing crimes motivated by bias against transgender individuals.

The regulation on aggravating circumstances is codified in BrB, Chapter 29, Section 2, Paragraph 7:

> As aggravating circumstances when assessing penalty value, in addition to what applies for each specific type of offence, particular consideration is given to:
>
> ...
>
> 7. whether a motive for the offence was to insult a person or a population group on grounds of race, colour, national or ethnic origin, religious belief, sexual orientation or transgender identity or expression, or another, similar circumstance.
>
> (Act 2019: 839)

The inclusion of *similar circumstance* in the regulation allows for a broader interpretation than the explicitly listed grounds. While this theoretically opens the possibility of including gender under the scope of the provision, there is no practical evidence to suggest that such an interpretation has been applied in legal practice.

Examples of crimes potentially falling under the regulation on aggravating circumstances

Below is a list of crimes committed online with anti-gender motive that could fall under the regulation of aggravating circumstances above. It is important to note that if the motive behind the crime targets a person's sexual orientation or transgender identity or expression, it may qualify as a hate crime under BrB, Chapter 29, Section 2, Paragraph 7. However, if the motive stems from other anti-gender biases – such as opposition to sex, gender, feminism, or gender equality – the crime may still be punishable under other legal provisions. In such cases, while the act may constitute a criminal offence, it would not legally be classified as a hate crime under the current regulation on aggravating circumstances. It is worth noting that a legislative process is currently underway proposing the inclusion of sex and gender as grounds for aggravating circumstances, as outlined below.

Defamation

The crime of defamation is regulated in BrB, Chapter 5, Section 1:

> A person who identifies someone as being criminal or as having a reprehensible way of life, or otherwise provides information liable to expose that person to the contempt of others is guilty of *defamation* and is sentenced to a fine.
>
> If they were obliged to make a statement or if, in view of the circumstances, it was otherwise justifiable to provide information about the matter, and if they show that the information was true or that they had reasonable grounds for it, they are not held responsible.

The second paragraph is establishing the border between the right to respect and dignity and the freedom of expression in these situations. As explained above, a hate motive allows a prosecutor to initiate proceedings for the offence, which would otherwise fall under private prosecution.

Insulting behaviour

The offence is regulated in BrB, Chapter 5, Section 3:

> A person who, in cases other than those referred to in Section 1 or 2, directs accusations, a derogatory statement or humiliating conduct at another person is, it the act is liable to violate the other person's self-esteem or dignity, guilty of *insulting behavior* and is sentenced to a fine.

Unlawful threat

Unlawful threat is criminalised under BrB, Chapter 4, Section 5:

> a person who threatens another person with a criminal act in a manner that is liable to occasion serious fear in the person threatened for the safety of their own or someone else's person, property, liberty or peace is guilty of making an unlawful threat and is sentenced to a fine or imprisonment for at most one year.
>
> (Act 2018: 1745)

The regulation was recently amended. Prior to the change in 2018, the offence applied only to threats against life, health, or property. Following criticism regarding gaps in the criminal legislation addressing online gender-based harassment, threats, and other violent acts, the law was revised. The current offence now includes situations where, for example, someone threatens to spread intimate images of another person – a scenario that previously did not fall under criminalisation.

Molestation

According to BrB, Chapter 4, Section 7:

> A person who physically molests another person or subjects another person to disturbing contact or other ruthless conduct, is, if the act is liable to noticeable vilate that person's peace, guilty of molestation and is sentenced to a fine or imprisonment för at most one year.
>
> (Act 2017: 1136)

Historically, the criminalisation of molestation addressed only physical acts. However, in 2018, the regulation was amended to include situations occurring online, reflecting the growing recognition of digital environments as spaces where such offenses can also take place. The example that opens the book, featuring a highly violent statement directed at a female journalist, fell outside the scope of this regulation prior to the legal amendment, according to the Court of Appeal. However, it could potentially be applicable under the current wording of the law.

Sexual molestation

When the molestation is of sexual character, another offence may be applicable, as regulated in BrB, Chapter 6, Section 10, Paragraph 2:

> This also applies to a person who exposes themselves to another person in a manner that is liable to cause discomfort, or who otherwise molests a person by word or deed in a way that is liable to violate that person's sexual integrity.
>
> (Act 2005: 90)

The provision on sexual molestation criminalises words and actions of a sexual nature that typically violate the victim's sexual integrity. It does not need to be proven in the individual case that the integrity was in fact violated. However, it has been emphasised that sexual molestation encompasses only actions with a clear sexual intent. This means that the perpetrator must have had a sexual interest in carrying out the act (prop. 2012/13: 111). The starting point for what constitutes sexual molestation is bodily contact. Inappropriate or unwanted touching of someone's breasts, buttocks, or crotch is clearly considered molestation intended to violate the other person's sexual integrity, but the provision may also include non-physical violations such as photographing, filming, comments, and similar acts. However, the question of whether non-physical actions fall within the scope of the provision remains under discussion (e.g. SOU 2010: 71, p. 381; Andersson & Wegerstad 2017/18) and review by the Supreme Court. It appears that non-physical actions, of which the victim is aware, may be considered to fall within the criminalised area (e.g. NJA 2017 s. 393).

Unlawful breach of privacy

Following debate and criticism, a new offence was introduced in 2018, that is, unlawful breach of privacy, regulated in BrB, Chapter 4, Section 6c. This crime targets image-based sexual abuse among other violations of a person's privacy.

> A person who intrudes into the private life of another person by disseminating:
>
> 1. An image of or other information about a person's sexual life;
> 2. An image of or other information about a person's state of health;
> 3. An image of or other information about a person being subjected to an offence that includes an attack on their person, liberty or peace;
> 4. An image of a person in a very vulnerable situation; or
> 5. An image of a person's wholly or partially naked body.
>
> If the dissemination is liable to result in serious damage to the person whom the image or information concerns, the offender shall be sentenced for unlawful breach of privacy and is sentenced to a fine or imprisonment for at most two years.
>
> (Act 2017: 1136)

Prior to the introduction of this provision, courts struggled to identify a suitable legal basis for punishing actions such as the distribution of images with nude or sexual content. In some cases, such actions could be classified as defamation, but this was not always applicable (Schultz 2013).

6.2.1.3 *Constitutional acts*

Some of the most serious offences mentioned above may also fall under the category of Offences against the Freedom of Expression Act. This classification provides the actions with stronger constitutional protection and alters the criminal procedure, as outlined in the introduction to this section.

The offences regulated under YGL, Chapter 7, Section 2, include unlawful threats, defamation, insulting behaviour, incitement to commit a crime, agitation against a population group, and unlawful depiction of violence (as criminalised in BrB, see above).

> The Chancellor of Justice may, in cases involving technical recordings, delegate to a public prosecutor the authority to act as prosecutor in freedom of expression cases concerning liability or confiscation on grounds

> of unlawful threats, agitation against a population group, unlawful depiction of violence, threats against a public servant, perversion of justice, or offences against civil liberties.
>
> However, the right to initiate public prosecution may not be delegated in cases concerning the freedom of expression offences of agitation against a population group or offences against civil liberties.
>
> (Act 2018: 1802)

These offences are regulated both under YGL, as above, and as Offences against the Freedom of Press Act under TF (Chapter 7 in this Act has its own definitions of the offences). The provisions are regulating the criminal responsibility for editors, and, are going through a different criminal procedure with a jury trial of nine members instead of a regular procedure in public court. The Chancellor of Justice is the only one that can initiate and pursue prosecution in cases concerning offences against the freedom of the press (TF Chapter 9, Section 2). The offences listed in the provision cited above are defined in BrB, with the distinction that it applies exclusively to acts carried out through media protected under constitutional provisions. This regulation is only applicable in specific online situations, such as when statements are published in the online edition of a newspaper or on a website with a valid publication license (YGL Chapter 1; TF Chapter 1). The introductory example in this chapter illustrates that constitutionally protected freedom of expression and freedom of the press enjoys stronger legal safeguards, and prosecutions under these fundamental laws rarely result in convictions.

6.2.1.4 Liable subjects

The question of criminal responsibility will be examined, encompassing not only the offender himself but also other potentially liable subjects, such as individuals responsible for overseeing discussions on electronic bulletin boards (including social platforms or specific sections of such platforms) and publishers in media-related cases.

Under Swedish criminal law, only individuals – not entities or groups – can be held liable for their actions. Crimes committed online may impose liability on the following parties:

1. The individual who made the statement, posted the image, or engaged in similar actions; or
2. The individual responsible for moderating the webpage or discussion platform where the speech act or similar content was posted; or
3. If the content was posted in a comment section belonging to a newspaper or website with a publication license (*utgivningsbevis*), the editor of that newspaper or website.

It should be noted that categories 1 and 2 fall outside the scope of constitutional regulation, while category 3 pertains specifically to the rules governing who may be held liable under the constitutional framework.

The individual perpetrator

The individual who committed the act is the primary subject to be held liable, both under criminal law and for civil compensation claims. However, there are additional mechanisms to establish criminal liability beyond the direct offender.

Responsibility for electronic bulletin boards

Lag (1998:112) om ansvar för elektroniska anslagstavlor (The Act on Responsibility for Electronic Bulletin Boards) establishes criminal liability for those who provide such platforms. An electronic bulletin board is defined as a program enabling communication, which may take the form of text, images, sound, or other types of information (prop. 1997/98: 15, p. 6). Examples include web hosting services, chat forums, discussion forums, comment sections, and similar platforms (prop. 1997/98: 15, p. 9; Forsman 2014, 140).

The law imposes obligations to supervise communications and to remove content that clearly constitutes specific offences. The person responsible is either the one who determines the platform's use or the one managing its operation (prop. 1997/98: 15, p. 10; Forsman 2014, 190). The obligation to monitor communications is assessed based on what is reasonable, considering the scope and nature of the activities (prop. 1997/98: 15, p. 15).

The crimes covered under this law include unlawful threats and unlawful breaches of privacy (both implemented 1 September 2018), as well as incitement to commit a crime, agitation against a population group, unlawful depiction of violence, and child pornography (see Sections 5 and 7 of the Act).

Liability of editors for press crimes

Under Swedish law, editors can be prosecuted for Offences under the Freedom of Expression Act or under the Freedom of the Press Act through a distinct criminal procedure. Only a limited number of specific acts qualify as such offences (see the section on Constitutional Acts above). Prosecution in these cases is, as explained above, exclusively conducted by the Chancellor of Justice, and trials are held with a jury consisting of nine members (see Chapter 12 of TF and Chapter 9 of YGL). In addition to the court system, there is an independent authority established by press organisations that evaluates cases according to its own ethical rules (The Media Ombudsman n.d.).

Criminal offences

6.2.1.5 Policies and legal proposals

The part of the GENHA reports dealing with state and local policies covers a range of subject matters connected to anti-gender (sexist) hate speech these include the Swedish gender equality policy, national plans to address racism and hate crime, national strategies to combat men's violence against women, initiatives to strengthen resistance to online hate, and actions to counter violent extremism. This broad field of policies involves various actors, including public authorities, regions or municipalities, and NGOs (Antigona Research Group 2020; see also Bladini 2020).

In early 2024, the Swedish government announced the strengthening of efforts to combat racism and hate crimes by initiating work on a new action plan. To complement the current action plan, five specific programmes have also been introduced, addressing different forms of racism: Afrophobia, antisemitism, anti-Gypsyism, Islamophobia, and racism against the Sámi people. The purpose of these programmes is to highlight the distinct manifestations of various types of racism (Skr. 2024/25: 60).

In 2024, the Swedish government announced a series of initiatives aimed at enhancing its gender equality policies. A central focus was placed on improving the governance and effectiveness of these policies through better indicators and strategic measures, especially in light of societal shifts such as digital transformation and labour market changes. In addition to this overarching initiative, the government continues its efforts to combat domestic violence and honour-based violence through preventative measures and protection for victims, incorporating tailored action plans for specific forms of violence (Regeringskansliet 2024a). The six overarching objectives of Sweden's gender equality policy remain central, encompassing equal distribution of power, economic equality, health equity, and the reduction of men's violence against women (Skr. 2016/17:10). A special investigator is appointed to evaluate the effectiveness of five of these objectives (excluding violence against women, which is subject to separate inquiry) in November 2024. Her work aims to propose updated indicators and strategies to address structural inequalities. Together, these efforts reflect Sweden's commitment to maintaining progressive and responsive gender equality frameworks (Regeringskansliet 2024a).

The Swedish government has reinforced its commitment to combating domestic violence and honour-based violence, recognising these as serious violations of human rights. As stated in official communication: Men's violence against women, domestic violence, honour-based violence and oppression, as well as prostitution and human trafficking, must be addressed comprehensively across all sectors of society. The 2024–2026 action programme encompasses 132 measures (Regeringskansliet n.d.). In 2024, efforts were intensified through the development of tailored action plans specifically targeting honour-related violence and oppression. These measures combine prevention, support, and protection, particularly for vulnerable groups, with an emphasis on improving coordination between public agencies and civil society organisations. Specific initiatives include strengthening support services for victims, improving legal frameworks, and increasing awareness and education about honour-based practices. By integrating these comprehensive approaches, the government aims to reduce the prevalence of such violence and to safeguard the rights and dignity of those affected (Regeringskansliet n.d.).

Sweden held the presidency of the Nordic Council of Ministers in 2024 and focused on issues related to honour-based violence and oppression, including work with LGBTQI+ individuals and economic gender equality (Regeringskansliet 2024b).

As part of this broader agenda, the government has strengthened legal protections against gender-based violence and discrimination. On 24 February 2022, it commissioned an inquiry to review the criminal justice system's safeguards against sexual violations. The investigation was tasked with evaluating the inclusion of gender as a new aggravating circumstance in hate crime legislation, as well as assessing whether protections for older individuals and other vulnerable groups require enhancement (SOU 2023: 80). On 15 October 2024, the Minister of Justice announced the findings, highlighting the severity of crimes motivated by gender-based hatred and their detrimental impact on democratic discourse (Regeringskansliet 2024c). The inquiry proposed adding gender as a basis for aggravating circumstances in the Swedish Penal Code's hate crime provisions (SOU 2023: 80).

The Minister further emphasised the importance of these measures in addressing the growing prevalence of sexualised hate rhetoric, which disproportionately targets women. The government has welcomed the inquiry's recommendations, recognising them as a vital step in strengthening protections for vulnerable women. With positive feedback from referral bodies, work is now underway to draft a legislative proposal for the Council on Legislation, signalling significant progress in Sweden's commitment to combating gender-based violence (Regeringskansliet 2024c).

6.2.2 Italy

The Italian Parliament ratified and implemented the International Convention on the Elimination of All Forms of Racial Discrimination (ICERD) through the so-called Reale Law (n°654, 17th October 1975). Subsequently, the so-called Mancino Law (n°205, 23rd June 1993) was enacted, incorporating offences such as propaganda, instigation, incitement, provocation, and discrimination based on racial, ethnic, national, or religious grounds into the Criminal Code (article n°604-bis). It also introduced the aggravating circumstance for offences motivated by ethnic, national, racial, or religious hatred (article n°604-ter).

However, these provisions do not include sexuality, sex or gender as protected categories. As a result, discriminations or violence against LGBTQI+ persons cannot be prosecuted under these laws due to the prohibition of applying the analogy principle in criminal law (according to the principle of legality). Consequently, such cases can only rely on the aggravating circumstance of an 'abject intents' in the Criminal Code (Commissione straordinaria per il contrasto dei fenomeni di intolleranza, razzismo, antisemitismo e istigazione all'odio e alla violenza 2022).

Efforts to amend articles n°604-bis and 604-ter of the Criminal Code have been ongoing (Sette 2024), driven by the recognition that these provisions were drafted in an era that did not foresee the challenges of online incitement to hatred. Nonetheless, any expansion of the scope of punishable speech must be accompanied by clear legal definitions in order to avoid conflating hate speech with other criminal acts, such as online harassment, which may have distinct motivations, objectives and legal foundations (Commissione straordinaria per il contrasto dei fenomeni di intolleranza, razzismo, antisemitismo e istigazione all'odio e alla violenza 2022).

One significant attempt to address this gap was the draft law (A.C. 569), presented to the Justice Commission of the Chamber of Deputies on 2 May 201 by MP Alessandro Zan and others. The draft sought to extend the scope of articles n°604-bis and 604-ter of the Criminal Code to include discrimination based on sex, gender, sexual orientation, gender identity, and disability. However, the proposal lacked clear definitions for the terms 'sexual orientation' and 'gender identity'.

Beyond enforcement, the draft law introduced primary and secondary prevention strategies. Article n°8 proposed measures targeting education, employment, security, and the prison system, as well as communication and media, all aimed at fostering awareness and inclusivity regarding sexual orientation and gender identity.

The draft law faced significant opposition from Parliament and parts of civil society. Initially scheduled for approval in July 2020, it was delayed, eventually returned to the Chamber of Deputies on 20 October 2020. Hundreds of obstructive amendments postponed the debate to 4 November 2020, when the law was approved in its first reading. However, during the Senate sittings on 27 October 2021, a secret ballot resulted in a decision to halt the examination of the draft articles. This effectively ended the legislative process, requiring any future effort to restart from the beginning after a mandatory six-month waiting period (Sodano 2021).

On 23 January 2023, a new draft law similar to the previously rejected proposal was presented to the Second Justice Commission. However, this draft has not yet been discussed.[7]

In addition, on 10 March 2021, another draft law was introduced to the Chamber of Deputies, focusing on measures to combat and prevent the dissemination of hate speech on the internet.

This proposal aims to increase accountability among digital platforms by obliging them to detect and remove illicit content, such as hate speech, at an early stage. Failure to comply would result in significant fines of up to 5 million euros. At the same time, the draft law seeks to balance enforcement with adequate procedural safeguards to ensure private enforcement mechanisms do not disproportionately restrict users' freedom of expression.

Despite its ambitions, the parliamentary debate on this draft has yet to commence (Tuzza 2024).

6.2.3 Spain

Article 510 of the Spanish Criminal Code, which defines hate crimes, was revised in 2015[8] to include sex, sexual identity or orientation and gender (among other sources of discrimination), among other grounds. Traditionally, the definition of hate speech required an imminent risk and/or use of violence, and a the victim belonged to a protected a group. However, the new provision defines hate speech as an attack on human dignity of a group or of an individual belonging to such a group, based on sex, sexual identity or orientation and gender (or other protected characteristics).

Article 510 of the Criminal Code include:

1. The following shall be punished with a prison sentence of one to four years and a fine of six to twelve months:
   a) Those who publicly encourage, promote or incite, directly or indirectly, hatred, hostility, discrimination or violence against a group on the grounds of … sex, sexual orientation or identity, gender … .
   b) Those who produce, elaborate, possess for the purpose of distributing, providing third parties with access, distributing, disseminating or selling writings or any other kind of material or supports that, due to their content, are suitable to encourage, promote, or directly or indirectly incite the hatred, hostility, discrimination or violence against a group … on the grounds of sex, sexual orientation or identity, gender … .
   c) Publicly deny, seriously trivialize or extol crimes of genocide, crimes against humanity or against persons and property protected in the event of armed conflict, or extol their perpetrators, when they have been committed against a group or part of it, or against a person determined by reason of their membership in the same … on the grounds of sex, sexual orientation or identity, gender … .
2. They will be punished by imprisonment from six months to two years and a fine from six to twelve months:
   a) Those who harm the dignity of people through actions that involve humiliation, contempt or discredit of any of the groups referred to in the previous section, or of a part of them, or of any person determined by reason of their membership in them
   b) Those who praise or justify by any means of public expression or dissemination the crimes that have been committed against a group, a part of it, or against a specific person by reason of their belonging to that group …

3. The penalties provided for in the previous sections will be imposed in the upper half when the events have been carried out through a social communication medium, through the Internet or through the use of information technologies, so that, that was made accessible to a large number of people.

Beyond the criminalisation of anti-gender hate speech, in 2022 it was adopted a new law on sexual freedom, the Organic Law 10/2022, of 6th September, of integral guarantee of sexual freedom. Although this law did not modify or add any aspect on the criminalisation of anti-gender hate speech, it defined digital violence as a form of sexual violence (article 3), and this has had consequences in the preventive and victim-focused approach of this law. Most of the law is dedicated to provide compensation to the victims of sexual violence and the re-establishment and effective protection of their rights.

Two other important laws were recently adopted in the field of anti-discrimination law, both containing provisions relevant to anti-gender hate speech. Law 15/2022, of 12 July, on equal treatment and non-discrimination, defines in Article 6.4 *discriminatory harassment* as behaviour that is intended to, or has the effect of, attacking the dignity of an individual or a group, on the grounds of sex, sexual orientation, sexual identity, gender expression, thereby creating an intimidating, hostile, degrading, humiliating or offensive environment.

Law 4/2023 of 28th of February, on the real and effective equality of trans people and the guarantee of the LGTBI rights, includes a similar provision in article 3d) *defining discriminatory harassment* as behaviours that aims to, or has the effect of, attacking the dignity of LGTBI individuals, and creating an intimidating, hostile, degrading, humiliating or offensive context.

In both laws, the legal procedures to address discriminatory harassment include administrative measures aimed at providing financial compensation to victims, and empowering public authorities to put an end to such discriminatory practices.

6.3 Concluding remarks

Online gender-based hate speech represents a pervasive challenge, emerging as a byproduct of the global digital landscape where communication is constant and unbounded. While European and international regulations, including the Council of Europe's instruments and the EU's recent initiatives, have sought to address this issue, the implementation of these frameworks at the national level reveals significant disparities.

Criminal law, though a powerful tool for addressing hate speech, struggles to keep pace with the rapidly evolving nature of online communication. The inherent inertia of legal systems, as well as the limited scope of national legislation, exacerbates the difficulty of addressing anti-gender hate speech comprehensively. Offences committed online often present procedural challenges, such as difficulties in identifying the user of an anonymous account or determining the person behind the screen. In Sweden, however, there is an alternative mechanism for establishing liability in some of the more serious cases. This involves holding the individual responsible for moderating the webpage or similar platform accountable, in accordance with standards that reflect the platform's size (e.g. the number of users). In addition, Sweden has made progress by incorporating hate motives, including sexual orientation and transgender identity, into its hate crime legislation. It is worth noting, however, that a legislative proposal to address this gap is currently under consideration. Meanwhile, Italy's legislative efforts to expand protections under its criminal code have faced strong resistance, delaying progress and leaving significant gaps in safeguarding vulnerable groups.

In Spain, hate speech is regulated in the Criminal Code, and in 2015 its scope was expanded to include protections on the grounds of sex and gender. However, convictions for hate speech against women remain rare, as these provisions are predominantly applied to hate speech targeting individuals based on sexual orientation or gender identity. While specific legislation on gender violence does not explicitly address anti-gender hate speech, the recent Law on Sexual Freedom (Organic Law 20/2022) included digital violence as a form of sexual violence, focusing primarily on victim support services rather than criminal liability. Civil remedies, though available, remain underutilised due to financial and procedural barriers, leaving significant gaps in addressing online anti-gender hate speech.

Finally, it is crucial to acknowledge the risks of misusing legal tools meant to combat hate speech. In Spain, for example, the interpretation of hate speech legislation as addressing 'intolerance' rather than 'discrimination' has led to cases being brought against feminists and activists defending themselves from sexist, homophobic, or xenophobic attacks online. This phenomenon underscores the dual-edged nature of criminal law, which, when misapplied, can harm the very individuals it seeks to protect. As such, any framework addressing anti-gender hate speech must carefully balance the need for protection with safeguards against potential misuse.

A unified approach, fostering collaboration between Member States and supporting civil society, is essential for addressing online anti-gender hate speech effectively. This includes not only strengthening legal frameworks but also investing in education, raising awareness, and promoting responsible digital platform governance. Without such concerted efforts, the gap between legal intent and practical enforcement will persist, undermining the broader fight against gender-based violence and discrimination.

Notes

1 The first recommendation from the Committee of Ministers on Hate Speech from 1997 (Recommendation no. 20 of 1997 on hate speech) focused on xenophobia and racism, and other recommendation from 2001 focuses on racism and xenophobia

in cyberspace (Recommendation 1543 (2001)). Following a timeline, it is worth mentioning a resolution on homophobia in Europe (from the European Parliament) from 2006 and a recommendation from CoE in 2010 (CM/Rec (2010)5) on measures to combat discrimination on grounds of sexual orientation or gender identity.
2 For an overview of the legislation, see Antigona Group (2020).
3 For a broader discussion on hate speech, see Buyse (2014); Brown (2015); and Heinze (2016).
4 For a further discussion, see Barker and Jurasz (2020).
5 Brottsförebyggande rådet (2017: 16).
6 Preparatory works, see prop. 1986/87: 151; KU 1987/88: 36; prop. 1970: 87, 1LU 1970:41, prop. 1981/82:58, JuU 1981/82:41, prop. 2001/02: 59, 2001/02:KU23, 2002/03:KU7 and prop. 2017/18:59, 2017/18:KU14.
7 Parlamento Italiano (2022), Lavori preparatori dei progetti di legge. www.camera.it/leg19/126?tab=&leg=19&idDocumento=401&sede=&tipo=.
8 By the Organic Law 1/2015 of 30th March, which modifies the Organic Law 10/1995 of 23rd November of the Criminal Code.

References

Literature

Andersson, U. & Wegerstad, L. (2017/18), 'Det kriminaliserade området för sexuellt ofreedande – kroppslig och abstrakt integritet'. *Juridisk tidskrift*, 3, 652–661.

Antigona Research Group (2020), *Report on the state of the art on anti-gender hate speech.* https://cris.unibo.it/retrieve/e1dcb335-f518-7715-e053-1705fe0a6cc9/REPORT%20ON%20THE%20STATE%20OF%20THE%20ART%20ON%20ANTI%20GENDER%20HATE%20SPEECH.pdf.

Antigona Research Group (2021), *Map of the main political parties using hate speech against the 'ideology of gender' through the social networks and internet in Europe.* https://ddd.uab.cat/pub/infpro/2021/250924/Map_of_the_main_political_parties_using_hate_speech_against_the_ideology_of_gender_through_the_social_networks_and_internet_in_Europe.pdf.

Barker, K. & Jurasz, O. (2019), *Online misogyny as hate crime: A challenge for legal regulation?* 1st ed. Routledge. https://doi.org/10.4324/9780429956805.

Belloni, P. (2024), 'The proposal for a directive in gender-based violence', *Media Laws.* www.medialaws.eu/the-proposal-for-a-directive-on-gender-based-violence/.

Bladini, M. (2020), 'Silenced voices. Online violence targeting women as a threat to democracy', *Nordic Journal on Law and Society*, 3(2), 1–42.

Brottsförebyggande rådet (2017), *Hatbrott 2016, Statistik över polisanmälningar med identifierade hatbrottsmotiv och självrapporterad utsatthet för hatbrott.* https://bra.se/download/18.3808406a192bd2f0b729140/1730807868250/2017_11_Hatbrott_2016.pdf (accessed 2024-12-01).

Brown, A. (2015), *Hate speech law: A philosophical examination.* Routledge.

Buyse, A. (2014), 'Dangerous expression: The ECHR, violence and free speech', *International & Comparative Law Quarterly*, 63(2), 491–503.

Forsman, M. (2014), *Internetpublicering och sociala medier: en juridisk vägledning.* Norstedts juridik.

Ganetz, H., Hansson, K. & Sveningsson, M. (Eds.) (2022), *Maktordningar och motstånd. Forskarperspektiv på #metoo i Sverige.* Nordic Academic Press.

Granström, G., Mellgren, C, and Tiby, E. (2016), Hatbrott? (1st Ed.) Studentlitteratur.

Heinze, E. (2016), *Hate speech and democratic citizenship*. Oxford University Press.

Lillian, D. L. (2017), 'A thorn by any other name: Sexist discourse as hate speech', *Discourse & Society*, 18, 719–740.

McGlynn, C. (2023), 'Criminalization at the margins: Downblousing, creepshots and image-based sexual abuse'. In *The criminalization of violence against women*. Oxford University Press.

NoHate (n.d.), 'No hate speech youth movement campaign'. ww.nohate.se/ (accessed 2024-11.27).

Öberg, J. (2024), 'The normative foundations for EU criminal justice'. In *Powers, limits and justifications*. Hart.

Schultz, M. (2013), *Näthat – rättigheter och möjligheter*. Karnov Group.

Sette, R. (2024), 'Proprio per quello che si è'. In: Sette, R. & Sicurella, S. (Eds.), *Parole in libertà: hate speech online attraverso l'Europa. Una lettura socio-criminologica*. Varazze: PM Edizioni, 13–45. E-book: www.pmedizioni.it/prodotto/parole-in-liberta-hate-speech-online-attraverso-leuropa/

Tiby, E. (1999), *Hatbrott? Homosexuella kcinnors och mäns berättelser om utsatthet för brott*. Stockholms universitet.

Tuzza, S. (2024), 'Iniziative di prevenzione e di contrasto all'odio online'. In Sette, R. & Sicurella, S. (Eds.), *Parole in libertà: hate speech online attraverso l'Europa. Una lettura socio-criminologica*. PM Edizioni. www.pmedizioni.it/prodotto/parole-in-liberta-hate-speech-online-attraverso-leuropa/.

Court cases

SWEDISH COURT CASES

Supreme Court, judgment in case NJA 2017 s. 393.

Public documents and laws

International (UN)

International Convention on the Elimination of All Forms of Racial Discrimination (ICERD), New York, 21 Dec. 1965, entered into force 4 Jan. 1969. www.ohchr.org/en/instruments-mechanisms/instruments/international-convention-elimination-all-forms-racial (accessed 2024-12-01).

UNESCO & Broadband Commission (2013). www.unesco.org/en/digital-policy-capacities-inclusion/broadband-commission (accessed 2024-11-27).

UN Women (2020), *The shadow pandemic: Violence against women during Covid-19*. www.unwomen.org/en/news/in-focus/in-focus-gender-equality-in-covid-19-response/violence-against-women-during-covid-19 (accessed 2024-11-26).

International (Council of Europe and EU)

Committee of Ministers (1997), *Recommendation no. R (97) 20 of the Committee of Ministers to Member States on 'Hate Speech'*. https://search.coe.int/cm#{%22CoEIdentifier%22:[%2209000016805 05d5b%22],%22sort%22:[%22CoEValidationDate%20Descending%22]} (accessed 2024-12-01).

Council of Europe (n.d.), *Convention on Cybercrime*, Budapest, 23.XI.2001. https://rm.coe.int/1680081561 (accessed 2024-12-01).

Council of Europe (2010), *Recommendation CM/Rec(2010)5 of the Committee of Ministers to member states on measures to combat discrimination on grounds of sexual orientation or gender identity*. www.coe.int/en/web/sogi/rec-2010-5 (accessed 2024-12-01).

Committee of Ministers (2022), *Recommendation CM/Rec(2022)16 20/05/22 of the Committee of Ministers to member States on combating hate speech*. www.coe.int/en/web/combating-hate-speech/recommendation-on-combating-hate-speech (accessed 2024-10-24).

Consolidated version of the Treaty on European Union (TEU)

Treaty on the Functioning of the European Union (TFEU)

Council Directive 2000/43/EC of 29 June 2000 *implementing the principle of equal treatment between persons irrespective of racial or ethnic origin*. https://eur-lex.europa.eu/legal-content/EN/TXT/PDF/?uri=CELEX:32000L0043 (accessed 2024-12-01).

Council of Europe (n.d.), *Combating hate speech*. www.coe.int/en/web/combating-hate-speech (accessed 2024-10-23).

Directive (EU) 2024/1385 of the European Parliament and of the Council of 14 May 2024 on *combating violence against women and domestic violence*. https://eur-lex.europa.eu/legal-content/EN/TXT/?uri=OJ%3AL_202401385 (accessed 2024-10-23).

European Commission against Racism and Intolerance (ECRI) (2015), *General Policy Recommendation no 15 on combating hate speech adopted on 8 December 2015*. https://rm.coe.int/ecri-general-policy-recommendation-no-15-on-combating-hate-speech/16808b5b01 (accessed 2024-10-23).

European Commission (n.d.), *Shaping Europe's digital future*. https://digital-strategy.ec.europa.eu/en/news/commission-calls-6-member-states-comply-eu-digital-servi ces-act (accessed 2024-12-01).

Parliamentary Assembly of the Council of Europe Resolution 2144 (2017), *Ending cyberdiscrimination and online hate*. https://pace.coe.int/pdf/f2ff807d63ea28f51 4f879949fb8f5dcc4dcce658a4758de922f6ac81d9881f2?title=Res.%202144.pdf (accessed 2024-12-01).

Sweden

Första lagutskottets utlåtande (ILU) nr bl år 1970: 41, *Utlåtande 1970:L1u41*. www.riksdagen.se/sv/dokument-och-lagar/dokument/utlatande/forsta-lagutskottets-utlatande-nr-bl-ar-1970_ft10l1u41/html/ (accessed 2024-12-02).

Justitieutskottets betänkande (JuU) 1981/82:41, *Om hets mot folkgrupp m.m.* https://data.riksdagen.se/fil/C44FCFB6-23AD-4B40-A75D-18919EAEC987 (accessed 2024-12-02)

Konstitutionsutskottets betänkande (KU) 1987/88: 36, *Om ändringar i tryckfrihetsförordningen*. www.riksdagen.se/sv/dokument-och-lagar/dokument/betankande/om-andringar-i-tryckfrihetsforordningen-m.m.-prop_gb01ku36/html/ (accessed 2024-12-02).

Konstitutionsutskottets betänkande 2001/02: KU23, *Hets mot folkgrupp, m.m.* www.riksdagen.se/sv/dokument-och-lagar/dokument/betankande/hets-mot-folkgrupp-m.m_gp01ku23/html/ (accessed 2024-11-27).

Konstitutionsutskottets betänkande 2002/03: KU7, *Hets mot folkgrupp, m.m.* www.riksdagen.se/sv/dokument-och-lagar/dokument/betankande/hets-mot-folkgrupp-m.m.-vilande_gq01ku7/html/ (accessed 2024-12-02).

Konstitutionsutskottets betänkande 2017/18: KU14, *Ett utvidgat straffrättsligt skydd för transpersoner.* www.riksdagen.se/sv/dokument-och-lagar/dokument/betankande/ett-utvidgat-straffrattsligt-skydd-for_h501ku14/html/ (accessed 2024-11-30).

Prop. 1948: 80, Kungl. Maj.ts proposition till riksdagen med förslag till lag om ändring i strafflagen m. m.; *given Stockholms slott den 20 februari 1948.* www.riksdagen.se/sv/dokument-och-lagar/dokument/proposition/kungl.-maj.ts-proposition-nr-80_e93080b1/html/ (Acccessed 2024-11-30).

Prop. 1970: 87, Kungl. Maj.ts proposition nr 87 år 1970 angående godkännande av konvention om avskaffande av rasdiskriminering, m. m.*; given Stockholms slott den 20 februari 1948.* www.riksdagen.se/sv/dokument-och-lagar/dokument/proposition/kungl.-maj.ts-proposition-nr-87-ar-1970_ft3087/html/ (accessed 2024-11-20).

Prop. 1981/82: 58, *om ändring i tryckfrihetsförordningen och brottsbalken (hets mot folkgrupp m.m.).* www.riksdagen.se/sv/dokument-och-lagar/dokument/proposition/om-andring-i-tryckfrihetsforordningen-och_g50358/html/ (accessed 2024-11-20).

Prop. 1986/87: 151, *om ändringar i tryckfrihetsförordningen m.m.* www.riksdagen.se/sv/dokument-och-lagar/dokument/proposition/om-andringar-i-tryckfrihetsforordningen-m.m_ga03151/html/ (accessed 2024-11-22).

Prop. 1987/88: 120, *om ändring i brottsbalken m.m. (straffmätning och påföljdsval m.m.).* https://data.riksdagen.se/fil/338B25F7-9835-4D5D-9F2E-83AA78D2BD1B (accessed 2024-12-10).

Prop. 1993/ 94: 101, *Åtgärder mot rasistisk brottslighet och etnisk diskriminering i arbetslivet.* www.riksdagen.se/sv/dokument-och-lagar/dokument/proposition/atgarder-mot-rasistisk-brottslighet-och-etnisk_gh03101/ (accessed 2024-12-01).

Prop. 1997/98: 55, *Kvinnofrid.* www.regeringen.se/contentassets/1733625e719c43b28f073fa9cdec90f2/kvinnofrid-prop.-19979855 (accessed 2024-11-27).

Prop. 2001/02: 59, *Hets mot folkgrupp, m.m.* www.riksdagen.se/sv/dokument-och-lagar/dokument/proposition/hets-mot-folkgrupp-m.m.-prop.-20010259_gp0359 (accessed 2024-12-01).

Prop. 2012/13: 111, *En skärpt sexualbrottslagstiftning.* www.regeringen.se/rattsliga-dokument/proposition/2013/03/prop.-201213111 (accessed 2024-12-01).

Prop. 2017/18: 59, *Ett utvidgat straffrättsligt skydd för transpersoner.* www.regeringen.se/rattsliga-dokument/proposition/2017/12/prop.-20171859 (accessed 2024-12-16).

Regeringskansliet (2024a), *Pressmeddelande från Arbetsmarknadsdepartmentet.* www.regeringen.se/pressmeddelanden/2024/11/uppfoljning-for-att-vassa-jamstalldhetspolitiken/ (accessed 2024-08-20).

Regeringskansliet (2024b), *Sveriges program för Nordiska ministerrådet för jämställdhet och LGBTI (MR-JÄM).* www.regeringen.se/regeringens-politik/sveriges-ordforandeskap-i-nordiska-ministerradet-2024/sveriges-program-for-nordiska-ministerradet-for-jamstalldhet-och-lgbti-mr-jam/. (accessed 2024-10-22).

Regeringskansliet (2024c), *Interpellation Märta Stenevi, den 2024/25:38 Kön som ny grund för straffskärpning vid hatbrott.* www.riksdagen.se/sv/dokument-och-lagar/dokument/interpellation/kon-som-ny-grund-for-straffskarpning-vid-hatbrott_hc1038 (accessed 2024-12-16).

Regeringskansliet (n.d.), *Åtgärdsprogram mot mäns våld mot kvinnor, våld i nära relationer och hedersrelaterat våld och förtryck.* www.regeringen.se/regeringens-politik/arbetet-mot-vald-i-nara-relationer-och-hedersrelaterat-vald-och-fortryck/ (accessed 2024-10-22).

Skr. 2016/17:10, *Mål, makt och myndighet – feministisk politik för en jämställd framtid.*

Skr. 2024/25: 60, *Regeringens handlingsplan mot rasism och hatbrott.* www.regeringen.se/informationsmaterial/2024/12/handlingsplan-mot-rasism-och-hatbrott/ (accessed 2024-12-15).

SOU 1944: 69, *Straffrättskommitténs betänkande med förslag till lagstiftning om brott mot staten och allmänheten.* Kungl. Boktryckeriet P.A. Norstedt & Söner.

SOU 2010: 71, *Sexualbrottslagstiftningen – utvärderingen och reformförslag.* Fritzes Offentliga Publikationer. www.regeringen.se/contentassets/0272e569daf046ccbab965be531524e8/sexualbrottslagstiftningen---utvarderingen-och-reformforslag-hela-dokumentet-sou-201071/ (accessed 2024-11-28).

SOU 2023: 80, *Ett starkare straffrättsligt skydd – mot sexuella kränkningar, bedrägerier i vissa fall och brott med hatmotiv avseende kön.* Betänkande av Utredningen om barns skydd mot sexuella kränkningar samt vissa frågor om brott mot kvinnor och äldre. Elanders Sverige AB. www.regeringen.se/contentassets/e8ccf3b8d03c46db856bc850e8c453dc/ett-starkare-straffrattsligt-skydd--mot-sexuella-krankningar-bedragerier-i-vissa-fall-och-brott-med-hatmotiv-avseende-kon.-sou-202380 (accessed 2024-11-27).

Other sources

BBC (2024). www.bbc.com/news/articles/ckg2kz9kn93o (accessed 2024-08-28).

Commissione straordinaria per il contrasto dei fenomeni di intolleranza, razzismo, antisemitismo e istigazione all'odio e alla violenza (2022), *Report a conclusione dell'indagine conoscitiva su natura, cause e sviluppi recenti del fenomeno dei discorsi d'odio, con particolare attenzione all'evoluzione della normativa europea in materia.* Senato della Repubblica Italiana. ww.senato.it/service/PDF/PDFServer/DF/410798.pdf (accessed 2024-11-28).

European Parliament (2024), 'A new push for European democracy'. www.europarl.europa.eu/legislative-train/theme-a-new-push-for-european-democracy/file-extending-the-list-of-eu-crimes-to-gender-based-violence (accessed 2024-10-24).

The Media Ombudsman (n.d.). https://medieombudsmannen.se/english/ (accessed 2024-12-01).

Sodano, A. (2021), *DdL Zan affossato in Senato: cosa è successo.* www.leggioggi.it/ddl-zan-cose/ (accessed 2024-12-01).

Wikipedia (latest updated 2024), Cissi Wallin, https://sv.wikipedia.org/wiki/Cissi_Wallin (accessed 2025-02-24).

7 Anti-gender hate speech regulation revisited

We have in this book approached anti-gender hate speech as a democratic problem of general character and not only or mainly as a problem for those who are exposed to this kind of speech. We have shown that when certain individuals' or groups' possibilities to participate in conversations online are undermined and their voices silenced as a result of them being exposed to anti-gender hate speech, what is at stake is a one-sided and a non-diverse debate.

In this chapter we analyse the fragmented landscape characterising legal instruments and policies (Chapters 3–6) on anti-gender online hate speech out of a democratic perspective and with the theoretical and conceptual framework presented in Chapter 2. As shown, the phenomenon is complex, constantly evolving, and characterised by a dynamic interplay between technology, law, and culture. The technological development facilitates an individual or a group to disseminate hateful words, images or other expressions with devastating consequences for other individuals, groups, and the whole society. The outer limit for such expressions seems to be expanded over time and fertilising more hate and fear, despite intensified ambitions to counteract them with law and policies on global, European, and national levels. The ambitions on various levels are not always consistent. Also, attempts to condemn and counteract hate speech on a global or European level is not always mirrored in national jurisdictions. The balancing between various values and principles has local varieties. Law and policies correlate with culture and in our time, culture seems to be a site for negotiations with many possible truths to adhere to. The technology facilitates the consolidation of subcultures online and the cyber character of online communities make it difficult to mitigate the possibilities to do harm with law and policies. The blurred boundary between private and public actors, such as when privately owned platoforms are managed at the owners' discretion but used by politicians and other public actors, opens for challenges on various levels. Such a development puts at risk not only the harm done to individuals and groups, but also the foundations of democracy.

This harm targeting individuals, groups, and democracy is today acknowledged, especially by international bodies such as UN, Council of

DOI: 10.4324/9781003383062-7

Europe, and the EU, yet less on a national level. On a UN level, the regulations and guidelines are indeed obliging on a state level, but merely politically and morally rather than legally enforceable. The legislation from the European bodies is legally binding, but most often as a minimum standard. Anti-gender hate speech has primarily been handled in guidelines and recommendations, hence not legally binding for the member states, although we now see a development in the use of legally binding instruments. The recent arising ambitious actions to combat anti-gender hate speech from the international bodies are not yet met with the same enthusiasm at a national level.

However, since 2017, when the criminal legal regulation was scarce, at least in the Nordic countries (Bladini & Nordisk information för kunskap om kön 2017), measures have been taken. In 2018, criminal legal regulation in Sweden was changed to include several sexual and violent expressions online that had previously fallen outside the scope of criminal law. These expressions are part of what we recognise as anti-gender hate speech, but the extensions were restricted to these specific actions and were not part of the legislation regulating hate speech and hate crime. Additionally, there are still gaps in national regulations, although the newly adopted legislation from the EU calls for further actions. Recent changes aimed at protecting specific professional groups, for example, journalists and politicians who are seen as particularly important for democracy, have been adopted. This indicates that online hate speech is recognised as a threat to democracy. However, even though women in these professions are particularly exposed, hate speech based on gender is still not addressed. In Italy, specific provisions for protection of certain professional groups do not exist.

Given the development described above, it could be presumed that it is only a matter of time until anti-gender hate speech is fully recognised and dealt with legally also on a national level. However, it is necessary to be aware of both the inherent resistance that lies within the traditional gendered legal system and the growing resistance from anti-gender movements around the world. The concerns are relevant due to related issues throughout history. The criminalisation of sexual violence has been debated and resisted for decades (MacKinnon 1996, 2016; Leijonhufvud 2015). The backsliding on gender equality policies and the rise of anti-gender movements must be taken seriously (Council of Europe 2024).

7.1 Anti-gender hate speech impacts several of the democratic core principles

We claim that anti-gender hate speech can have a negative impact on democracy. Democracy, generally perceived as an ideal of inclusion and something to strive for, is not achieved if not all voices have access to be expressed and heard. Also, democracy requires that everyone has the same rights, opportunities, and power to form society and one's own life, which is what gender equality entails. Moreover, democracy requires an understanding of freedom of expression as two fold, not only as freedom from interventions in the form of censorship, but also as the guarantee of a diversity of voices. Measures to safeguard such diversity are necessary to foster a democratic society (Kenyon, Svensson & Edström 2017). The responsibility to secure this is not only a matter for individuals, but also for the state and other governing bodies.

Anti-gender hate speech collides with several core democratic principles. First, as has been shown, it may be discriminatory, as it is both gender-stereotypical and perceived as violence against women, thus counteracting the democratic *principle of gender equality*. Secondly, and as also shown, it may lead to the silencing of certain voices, thereby limiting of the *principle of freedom of expression*, understood not only as the individual right to express oneself, but also as diversity of voices and in the service of common good.

Most democracies emphasise the importance of active participation. *Fulfilling the participatory principle* presupposes not only the formal right to take part in political processes of all kinds, but also practical possibilities to do so. To reach a high level of participation, active measures are required to ensure that everyone can take part. Anti-gender hate speech has a negative impact on effective access to participation. Through hateful expressions, women are silenced and thereby hindered from participating in democratic processes. When participation is obstructed, it collides with the *egalitarian principle*. It is not only a matter of some voices being silenced, but also of limiting the overall ability to make informed decisions. Participation presupposes access to information and participation in public debate. It also requires a practical possibility to participate in, for example, policymaking. Systematic inequalities in access to participation in political and governing processes are among the effects of anti-gender hate speech. Therefore, it should be considered a duty of the state and other governing bodies to counteract anti-gender hate speech and thereby secure democracy.

The *deliberative principle*, another core democratic principle, requires public reasoning, a focus on the common good, and motivated political decisions, not merely an aggregation of existing preferences. A respectful dialogue at all levels, among informed and competent participants who are open to persuasion is also a prerequisite according to this principle. Anti-gender hate speech is often characterised by emotional appeals, parochial interests, and coercive tendencies, which may evoke emotions such as hatred and fear – rather than foster public reasoning oriented toward the common good and motivated political decisions. While individual responsibility to maintain a respectful dialogue is important, it is not sufficient, when individuals fail to uphold it. Regulation is one possible measure to ensure that the deliberative principle can be fulfilled.

The relationship between democracy, gender equality, and freedom of expression has been thoroughly explored in the previous chapters. This connection is recognised globally, as well as at European and national levels. Power – and the lack thereof – is a crucial element of this relationship. The example of Swedish gender equality has further illustrated this interplay.

It is evident that anti-gender hate speech constitutes a significant obstacle to achieving democracy. If contemporary democracies are to remain democracies, addressing and limiting anti-gender hate speech is imperative. The means to do so, however, are not self-evident. Nor is it clear which actors should assume responsibility. What is clear, though, is that states and other legislative bodies must be among those taking action.

7.2 Restriction or extension of freedom of expression

Are measures to counteract anti-gender hate speech to be understood as restrictions of freedom of expression or as extensions? Freedom of expression is, as said above, one of the most prominent principles in a democracy. Even the thinnest version of democracy (defined by V-Dem; see Chapter 2) embraces the importance of freedom of expression. Provisions on freedom of expression are commonly perceived as an individual right to express oneself, even though theories might acknowledge other justifications, such as the common good and being a means to achieve democracy. Any balancing in favour of another democratic principle is in most jurisdictions and by many people seen as a restriction of free speech. Thus, to act against anti-gender hate speech is commonly considered a restriction. Restrictions are, at least according to the same jurisdictions, legitimate if fulfilling certain requirements. The exceptions are to be clearly defined and considered to be as limited as possible.

However, what is also clear, although not always acknowledged, is that with freedom or rights comes responsibility. This responsibility implies that the use of such right must be subject to consideration. To be responsible indicates that, when taking action, its potential consequences should be considered. A richer perception of democracy as deliberative (like the Swedish democracy is said to be) presupposes a respectful dialogue as indicated above. To have a respectful dialogue means that the focus shifts from what is said to how something is said. It is not the ideas as such that are to be hindered but how they are communicated. To have concern about the counterpart and be careful about the communication is important for democracy. Having said that, it is not prohibited to express ideas 'that [...] offend, shock or disturb the State or any sector of the population' (*Handyside v. UK* 1976).

The view that any balancing is a restriction and that such restrictions may be justified, has been dominant and still is. This is understandable if the provisions, as for instance in Art. 19 ICCPR and Art. 10 ECHR, are taken into consideration. It is explicitly stated that the exercise of these rights may be subject to certain restrictions, if they are provided by law and are deemed necessary. Most theories offering justifications for freedom of expression however, provide a richer understanding of freedom of expression than just being an individual right to express oneself. The view of an individual right that ought to be protected from interventions by the state is too simplified. The theories of justification also emphasises its role for democracy at the societal level. If the purpose of freedom of expression is understood as serving democracy it becomes evident that promotion of a diversity of voices is also an essential aspect of freedom of expression. If democracy in a participatory and deliberative version is the aim, this must be safeguarded by the state or other regulative body. This view on freedom of expression, as encompassing both non-censorship and a diversity of voices, is explicitly established in the Swedish constitutional acts, as well as in statutes regulating public service and media. This view also characterises the Nordic countries more broadly.

In a time when freedom of expression is increasingly discussed almost exclusively as an individual right, it is important to remind ourselves of its role in ensuring that certain individuals or groups are not silenced by others. Actions taken to safeguard a diversity of voices should be understood as an extension of freedom of expression, not as a restriction. Such a view, that addressing hate speech does not equate to limiting or prohibiting freedom of speech, was recently affirmed by the UN in its Strategy and Plan of Action on Hate Speech from 2019.

Therefore, we challenge and question the perception that considerations favouring other democratic principles should be seen as restrictions. We suggest that they should instead be understood as an extension of freedom of expression. This means that in order to safeguard everyone's voices to be heard and to guarantee a diversity of voices, measures such as condemning the silencing of voices, ensuring heterogenous content in public service and other broadcasting actors, etc., are required. What has been labelled a Nordic Media Welfare State (Syvertsen et al. 2014), is characterised by such a safeguarding of a broad perception of freedom of expression. To counteract anti-gender hate speech, we claim, should therefore to be seen as an extension of freedom of expression.

7.3 Anti-gender hate speech in a patriarchal society

This section examines how anti-gender hate speech functions both as an expression of, and a mechanism within, a patriarchal order that has historically marginalised women's experiences and narratives. It seeks to explore the central question: how and why are we beginning to see shifts in the legal treatment of anti-gender hate speech across different levels of governance?

One of the central premises of this analysis is that law is inherently gendered (Svensson 1997; Conaghan 2013). Historically, the patriarchal system has shaped legal orders by privileging male perspectives while marginalising the voices and experiences of women and gender minorities. In this context, anti-gender hate speech is not merely a collection of isolated acts, but a reflection of a broader structure of power that sustains and enforces patriarchal dominance. This dual function of sexism – as the justification of patriarchy – and misogyny – as its enforcement – is a crucial lens for understanding how anti-gender hate speech operates within a patriarchal legal system (cf. Manne 2018).

Manne's concepts of himpathy and herasure provide a useful framework to understand the ways in which patriarchal law has continued to uphold these dynamics. Himpathy, as described in Chapter 2, refers to the systemic tendency to extend sympathy, leniency, and understanding to male perpetrators of gendered harm and violence. Herasure, on the other hand, describes the tendency to trivialise or neglect women's experiences and narratives, ensuring that their voices remain unheard, or not taken seriously. These concepts can be used to illustrate how and understand why anti-gender hate speech, as a manifestation of misogyny, has historically been excused or minimised under the guise of protecting freedom of expression – frequently understood from a male-dominated perspective.

This patriarchal bias is deeply entrenched in legal frameworks, where the right to express (misogynistic) views has often been prioritised over the need to safeguard a diversity of voices, including those advocating for gender equality (Svensson & Edström 2014, 2016; see also Kenyon, Svensson & Edström 2017). In many jurisdictions, the balancing of free expression against the harms caused by hate speech has disproportionately favoured the former, reflecting broader societal patterns of himpathy. At the same time, women's experiences of hate, harassment, and violence are commonly individualised and framed as isolated incidents rather than recognised as elements of a systemic pattern. Law seems to favour the individual and the specific action rather than the common good (ideas of the common good, a democratic debate and gender equality). Thus, we tend to reduce women's experiences, and see them as individual actions and not as elements of a pattern, contributing to herasure. This tendency, consistent with the traditional design of criminal law, obscures the structural nature of misogyny and its connection to other forms of violence against women.

However, a growing recognition of anti-gender hate speech as a democratic problem and as part of men's violence against women is emerging on the international, and European levels, as shown in Chapter 4 and 5. Over time, gender has been acknowledged as a basis for hate speech in international and regional instruments, such as the recommendations of the European Commission against Racism and Intolerance (ECRI) and the Istanbul Convention recognise a continuum between gender stereotypes, gender inequality, sexism and violence against women and girls. These frameworks reflect an evolving understanding of how anti-gender hate speech undermines democratic principles, including the right to participate in public discourse free from violence. On the European level, this transformation is evident in efforts to integrate gender into hate speech regulations, linking it explicitly to the broader struggle for gender equality. By framing anti-gender hate speech as a form of violence against women, these developments challenge the traditional, gendered legal order. Nevertheless, the implementation of these norms at the national level remains uneven, with Sweden providing a telling example.

In Sweden, although improvements have been made – particularly since 2018 in the area of anti-gender hate speech, including significant updates to criminal law protections for women (cf. Bladini & Nordisk information för kunskap om kön 2017; Bladini 2020) – gaps persist in recognising gender as a specific category within hate speech legislation. Proposals to introduce gender as an aggravating factor in sentencing represent an important step forward, not only in aligning Swedish law with international and European standards, but also as an expression of a broader shift in perspective. This proposal indicates an emerging tendency to view individual acts of gender-based hate or violence not merely as isolated incidents but as part of a larger structural pattern of misogyny. While this development signals progress, it also underscores the slow pace of legal adaptation and the challenges of integrating a structural understanding of gendered violence into the traditionally individualistic framework of criminal law. This delay reflects entrenched dynamics of herasure, where women's collective experiences of misogyny are minimised in favour of focusing on isolated incidents, and himpathy, which sustains leniency towards perpetrators by prioritising broader freedoms over gendered harm.

These gaps highlight the tension between international norms and their national implementation, reflecting deeper resistance to recognising the structural dimensions of gendered violence within patriarchal legal systems. Nevertheless, the increasing inclusion of gender in definitions of hate speech, and its framing as a democratic issue, suggests a growing challenge to the longstanding patriarchal order. While the direction of change is clear, these advances cannot be taken for granted. Across parts of the Western world, we are witnessing tendencies to roll back progress on gender equality, with fundamental rights and protections being questioned or actively undermined. These setbacks can be understood as manifestations of himpathy, where patriarchal systems continue to protect male-dominated structures, and herasure, which ensures that women's experiences and narratives remain marginalised in legal and public discourses. This underscores the importance of sustained vigilance and advocacy to ensure that the momentum towards addressing anti-gender hate speech and dismantling patriarchal structures is not lost.

7.4 The extension and persistence of what is hate speech

Has the scope of hate speech been extended over time and is it then only a matter of time until gender is included in all jurisdictions? Hate speech as a concept and as a behaviour has a history of embracing reprehensible behaviour directed exclusively against certain persons and groups on some specific grounds. New grounds have over time been added to what is included in the concept. It was originally targeted by legislation established after the World War II, due to experiences of hate propaganda performed by the nazis targeting Jews, Romans and other groups of people. Several European countries criminalised hate speech at that time based on ethnicity and the aim was to prevent resurgence of Nazism. For example, the crime called *hets mot folkgrupp* (literally translated to English: agitation against a population group) was adopted in Sweden in 1948. The first UN human rights instrument prohibiting certain 'propagation' and 'promotion of ideas' was the International Convention on the Elimination of All Forms of Racial Discrimination (ICERD) in 1965, if endorsed by public authorities or institutions concerning racial superiority or racial discrimination.

In many countries the scope of the crime has been gradually broadened and extended to more identity factors such as sexual orientation, religion and more recently to gender identity. There has been a gradual inclusion of sex/gender in hate speech regulation, both in policies and legal instruments, as shown in Chapter 6. For example, the UN Strategy and Plan of Action on Hate Speech from 2019 (United Nations 2019) includes gender and so does the definition by ECRI. The UN Strategy and Plan of Action mentions religion, ethnicity, nationality, race, colour, descent, gender *or other* identity factors. The list is obviously not closed to some but open to other factors that might be relevant to protect in the future. However, in some jurisdictions like the Swedish and Italian, sex and gender is not included in hate speech regulations.

Some of the arguments that have been used as excuses for not including sex or gender in hate speech regulation reflects a variety of underlying reasons. In a Swedish context, the argument that hate speech regulation is intended to protect minorities has been used, and since women as a group are not considered a minority, they should not be included. (Bladini & Nordisk information för kunskap om kön 2017). This can be compared to the Norwegian discussion, which takes a clear power perspective: and as women as a group hold less power than men, sex or gender can be included (Bladini & Nordisk information för kunskap om kön 2017). Another argument sometimes put forward is that it would not be practically feasible to include sex or gender, due to the number of cases that would be reported to the police. The police authority, it is claimed. would drown under the burden of cases. The argument, as dicsussed above, that freedom of expression should not be restricted may be the most commonly used. What could be added to the above is that the balancing between freedom of expression and gender equality should favour of freedom of expression is an example of herasure and himpathy. Women's experiences of anti-gender hate speech are not considered serious enough to justify a limitation of freedom of expression. Meanwhile, men's interest in saying whatever they want without restrictions is considered a legitimate reason to prioritise that interest.

The scope of grounds included in hate speech has clearly broadened over time. Still, a reluctance to include sex or gender remains apparent in several national jurisdictions. The ambitions of the UN, European and EU to address and eliminate hate speech targeting sex or gender may have an impact at the national level. So far, however, the driving forces mainly operate top-down, while some hesitance persist at the national level. One possible explanation is that it is easier, and less obliging, to formulate goals and ideals at the international, European and EU levels, than at the national level, where impementation must occur.

The tendency to include sex and gender in the definition of hate speech at the international and regional levels is essential. Also important is the use of EU directives requiring the Member states to implement them. A recent example is the Directive to prevent and combat gender-based violence, both online and offline (Directive (EU) 2024/1385). Instruments with transformative interpretation potential, such as CEDAW and the Istanbul Convention, are also important in placing demands on states to implement measures to combat anti-gender hate speech.

7.5 Small actions' enabling of the larger ones

This section examines how seemingly minor, everyday actions contribute to larger systemic issues, such as patriarchal structures, anti-gender hate speech, and gender-based violence. Drawing on feminist legal theory, we argue that these small acts, often trivialised as insignificant, are integral to the maintenance of broader systems of oppression. Central to this analysis is the question: how do these actions perpetuate structural inequality, and how can legal frameworks address their cumulative impact?

A key challenge in addressing anti-gender hate speech lies in the persistent distinction between speech and act. As discussed in Chapter 2, MacKinnon's (1996) critique of this dichotomy remains pivotal: speech is often dismissed as 'mere words' presumed incapable of constituting harm. This perspective overlooks the performative nature of language – its capacity to enact harm and sustain systems of control. Anti-gender hate speech exemplifies this dual nature. Everyday remarks dismissing gender equality or legitimising sexism are not merely reflective of misogynistic attitudes; they actively reinforce patriarchal power structures. For example, online memes that mock feminist advocacy or perpetuate 'jokes' about traditional gender roles serve to normalise hostility and validate broader ideologies of exclusion.

This understanding challenges the traditional privileges of free speech over the harms inflicted by hate speech, positioning it as an act with real and cumulative consequences. Speisel's (2024) exploration of the rhetorical strategies within hate speech, as noted earlier, underlines how seemingly innocuous expressions work to conceal their intent while reinforcing structural inequality. These patterns align with the everyday life perspective, which situates such acts within broader cultural practices.

Grounding this analysis in the everyday life perspective reveals how structural inequality is reproduced through daily interactions and norms. As critiqued by MacKinnon (2016) and Naffine (2002) the gap between legal abstractions and women's lived experiences creates barriers to justice. An everyday life perspective provides a framework for understanding how situational and relational dynamics shape autonomy and agency (Bladini & Svedberg Andersson 2020). This approach reveals how everyday acts – such as sexist remarks, microaggressions, or dismissive attitudes towards gender equality – are not isolated but form part of a broader cultural pattern that marginalises women and normalises hostility towards gender minorities.

This perspective underscores the limitations of narrow definitions of hate speech, often employed in legal context. These definitions typically focus on overtly harmful or criminalised expressions, such as explicit threats or incitement to violence. By incorporating the concept of 'hate speech potential', as highlighted in Fejős and Zentai (2021) we extend the scope to include both implicit and explicit forms. Subtle expressions of bias – such as derogatory jokes or seemingly innocuous comments about gender roles – contribute to a cultural environment that legitimises and enables more overt hostility (cf. Fejős & Zentai 2021) This broader view aligns with feminist critiques that emphasise the continuum of harm, wherein everyday expressions of hate and prejudice form the foundation for more severe acts of violence and exclusion.

Expanding on the conceptual framework offered by GENHA, this understanding situates even ostensibly minor actions within a broader spectrum of harm. At the ideological level, anti-gender hate speech often reflects deeply rooted conservative and nationalist beliefs, promoting a vision of society that marginalises gender equality and enforces traditional roles. At the discursive level, such expressions – including jokes, memes, and coded language – serve as strategic tools for normalising hostility while deflecting criticism. For example, far-right groups have effectively employed humour as a tactic, using memes to convey misogynistic or anti-gender messages in a veiled manner. This approach makes hateful content appear harmless, thereby trivialising its impact and embedding systemic misogyny within everyday discourse.

By recognising the cumulative and enabling effects of these acts, we can challenge the trivialisation of everyday hostility and emphasise its role in sustaining systemic inequality. This process of herasure, where the voices and experiences of women are marginalised or dismissed, is central to understanding how anti-gender hate speech functions within a patriarchal framework. Through this lens, we see how subtle, seemingly benign expressions of bias not only perpetuate structural misogyny but also create a permissive environment for more overt acts of hate and violence.

As discussed in Chapter 2, Kelly's (1988) continuum of violence provides a framework for understanding how these seemingly minor acts are interconnected with more severe forms of violence. This continuum has, in Sweden, been expanded through feminist scholarship and policy. Lundgren's (1993) theory of the normalisation of violence has influenced the Swedish criminal law. For example, the offence of gross violation of a woman's integrity recognises the cumulative impact of systemic abuse, such as controlling behaviours and repeated threats (Prop. 1997/98: 55). These legal advancements highlight how structural violence can be addressed by acknowledging the links between micro-level actions and systemic oppression.

The pyramid of violence, as conceptualised by Franzén and Gottzén (2020), further illustrates the need to address not only overtly criminal acts, but also their socially acceptable foundations. This logic underpins Sweden's gender equality policy, which aims to eliminate men's violence against women while promoting equal participation in public and economic life. This dual focus underscores how addressing systemic violence is integral to achieving broader societal goals.

Building on these frameworks, we propose the concept of *continuum of online anti-gender hate speech* as a form of gender-based violence. This continuum integrates the aforementioned ideas while expanding them in the following ways. First, hate speech is understood as a form of group injustice, targeting members of groups subjected to systemic discrimination in the context in which the speech occurs (Richardson-Self 2021: 56). While individuals are harmed directly, their harm is secondary and contingent upon their membership in these marginalised groups.

Second, anti-gender hate speech operates not only at the individual and group levels, but also on a structural societal level. It is embedded in and perpetuated by institutional practices, power dynamics, and cultural norms, that sustain misogynistic, conservative, and nationalist ideologies (cf. anti-gender movements literature, as discussed in the introduction). This speech both reflects and reinforces a broader cultural and political climate hostile to gender equality. Moreover, this structural dynamic is bidirectional. On the one hand, the spread of anti-gender rhetoric amplifies exclusionary ideologies; on the other hand, the silencing effect of hate speech constrains the participation of targeted groups in public discourse, undermining their participation in public and political life and perpetuating unequal access to democratic debate.

We argue that hate speech, as a form of gendered violence, profoundly shapes public debate by determining whose voices are amplified and whose are silenced. Through the lens of the everyday life perspective and the concept of the continuum of violence, we can map the interconnections between individual experiences, group-level exclusionary dynamics, and the overarching ideological and power structures that sustain these patterns. This framework reveals how anti-gender hate speech operates simultaneously on personal and systemic levels, reinforcing inequalities across social, political and cultural domains. By extending himpathy – the systemic tendency to empathise with and protect male-dominated perspectives – and herasure – the marginalisation and trivialisation of women's voices and experiences – we can further illustrate how anti-gender hate speech not only inflicts personal harm but also upholds structural inequalities. These dynamics ensure that patriarchal narratives dominate public discourse while silencing dissenting voices, thereby perpetuating systemic exclusion and undermining democratic participation.

Legal frameworks must evolve to address these cumulative harms. This requires moving beyond narrow definitions of hate speech to encompass its broader cultural and systemic dimensions. These theoretical foundations are increasingly reflected in legal frameworks at the international and EU levels, and are beginning to influence national policies, including in Sweden. The Swedish gender equality policy exemplifies this connection. The overarching goal – that everyone shall have the same power to influence society and their own life – is operationalised through several interrelated subgoals, including the elimination of gender-based violence and the promotion of equal participation in political and economic life.

These goals are mutually reinforcing: protecting women from violence is essential for enabling their full participation in the public sphere. By addressing the continuum of online anti-gender hate speech, we can identify its role as both a form of gender-based violence and a barrier to achieving gender equality, as it undermines women's ability to influence society and live free from fear and intimidation.

7.6 Legitimising criminalisation

The criminalisation of anti-gender hate speech is a contentious issue, requiring a careful balance between protecting individual freedoms and addressing structural inequalities. This analysis integrates the criminalisation principles of harm, common goods, and public wrong with the theoretical frameworks of the continuum of violence and the everyday life perspective. Together, these approaches illuminate how anti-gender hate speech operates across individual, group, and societal levels, perpetuating harm and reinforcing systemic exclusion. Concepts such as himpathy and herasure further illustrate how patriarchal structures influence not only the societal understanding of harm but also the conditions under which criminalisation is deemed justifiable. Central to this analysis is the question: how can the criminalisation of anti-gender hate speech online be legitimised within democratic frameworks, ensuring that it addresses structural harms while safeguarding the fundamental principles of freedom of expression and equality?

The harm principle provides a clear starting point for justifying the criminalisation of anti-gender hate speech. As discussed earlier, this principle traditionally focuses on direct harm to individuals, such as psychological damage caused by targeted harassment. However, as Feinberg (1984) emphasises, harm must be understood contextually, recognising how individual actions are embedded in broader patterns of violence. For example, recurring online harassment campaigns targeting women not only harm individuals but also contribute to a climate of fear, effectively silencing dissenting voices.

Expanding beyond individual harm, the principle of common goods emphasises the importance of protecting collective societal interests, such as equality and freedom of expression. For example, the normalisation of derogatory memes targeting feminists not only trivialises gender equality but also diminishes the quality of public discourse by legitimising exclusionary narratives. Criminalisation under this principle aligns with the need to ensure inclusive participation in the public sphere, recognising that democracy depends on the equal ability of all groups to contribute to societal debates.

Similarly, the concept of public wrongs extends the rationale for criminalisation to acts that harm the community as a whole. Anti-gender hate speech, by attacking shared values such as gender equality and pluralism, constitutes a wrong against the democratic order itself. This is particularly evident in the offence of agitation against a population group (*hets mot folkgrupp*) under Swedish criminal law, which addresses expressions that threaten the public interest in maintaining social cohesion. However, current national legislation often excludes gender as a protected category, leaving a significant gap in addressing systemic misogyny.

The principle of common goods also offers a lens to address the tension between criminalisation and freedom of expression. The duty to protect common goods, such as a pluralistic public discourse, justifies limiting speech that silences or marginalises vulnerable groups. For example, international frameworks such as the European Commission against Racism and Intolerance (ECRI) and the Istanbul Convention explicitly recognise gender-based hate speech as a threat to democratic participation, framing it as both a harm to individuals and an attack on societal values.

In this context, criminalisation serves as a safeguard for maintaining the balance between protecting free expression and preventing systemic exclusion. By addressing hate speech that disproportionately targets women and gender minorities, criminal law reinforces the principle that democracy thrives on the equal representation of diverse voices.

At the national level, legislation often focuses on isolated acts of hate speech, reflecting an emphasis on individual actions. For instance, laws against online harassment criminalise explicit threats or targeted abuse but may overlook subtler expressions, such as coded language or memes, that contribute to systemic harm. This approach aligns with the harm principle but risks neglecting the structural dimensions of hate speech.

In contrast, the inclusion of aggravating factors for gender-based hate crimes, as proposed in Sweden, begins to address the broader patterns of harm. By recognising the cumulative impact of such acts, this measure aligns with the continuum of violence, acknowledging how everyday hostility forms the foundation for more overt acts of exclusion and violence. Similarly, agitation against a population group (*hets mot folkgrupp*) could be expanded to include gender as a protected category, reflecting the principle of public wrongs by addressing hate speech as an attack on democratic values.

As we have shown, international legal frameworks increasingly address anti-gender hate speech from the perspectives of common goods and public wrongs. For example, the Istanbul Convention links hate speech to systemic gender inequality, framing it as a threat to societal cohesion and individual well-being. This approach highlights the structural dimensions of harm, recognising that hate speech undermines democratic values by marginalising certain groups.

However, national legal systems often remain rooted in a narrower, individualistic perspective, focusing on specific acts rather than systemic patterns. This divergence reflects the differing emphases of international and national legal cultures: while international frameworks aim to address collective harms and uphold shared values, national systems frequently prioritise individual accountability and intent. Bridging this gap requires aligning domestic legislation with international principles, ensuring that national laws address not only the direct harm caused by hate speech but also its structural and societal implications.

A consistent framework for criminalising anti-gender hate speech must integrate the principles of harm, common goods, and public wrongs. This involves recognising that hate speech operates across multiple levels – harming individuals, marginalising groups, and threatening societal values. By addressing these dimensions, criminal law can disrupt patterns of himpathy and herasure, challenging the patriarchal structures that sustain systemic inequality.

While criminalisation is not a panacea, its symbolic and normative functions make it an essential tool for fostering a more inclusive public sphere. In conjunction with complementary measures, such as education and restorative justice, criminal law can reinforce societal commitments to equality and democracy, ensuring that all voices are heard and valued.

The criminalisation of anti-gender hate speech online can be legitimised within democratic frameworks by balancing the principles of harm, common goods, and public wrongs. First, harm must be understood not only as immediate and individual but as cumulative and systemic, recognising the continuum of violence that connects everyday hostility to broader structural inequalities. By addressing hate speech as a form of gender-based violence that silences voices, and undermines participation, criminal law protects individuals and groups from both direct harm and the enabling environments that sustain it.

Second, the principle of common goods underscores the necessity of safeguarding democratic values, including gender equality and pluralism. Criminalising online hate speech that targets gender equality is not merely about protecting individuals but about preserving the integrity of public discourse, ensuring that all voices can participate free from intimidation or exclusion.

Finally, the principle of public wrongs provides a rationale for addressing hate speech as a threat to societal cohesion and democratic stability. By framing anti-gender hate speech as an attack on shared values, such as inclusivity and dignity, criminalisation affirms society's commitment to combating systemic discrimination. At the international level, frameworks like the Istanbul Convention exemplify how these principles can guide legal responses, even as national laws continue to grapple with the fragmented nature of online harm.

In sum, legitimising the criminalisation of anti-gender hate speech online requires a holistic approach that transcends individual intent to address systemic impacts. By integrating these principles with concepts such as himpathy, herasure, and the continuum of violence, criminal law can challenge patriarchal structures while reinforcing democratic ideals of gender equality, freedom, and participation. That said, one must remain attentive to the potential harms and structural biases inherent in the use of criminal law. A sustainable and effective response to anti-gender hate speech must include coordinated efforts in education, civil society, and digital governance.

7.7 A side question: A Nordic walk-over

Have the Nordic countries, and Sweden in particular, once role models for gender equality, fallen behind other countries? Given the Nordic context and gaze, which is our starting point, we will reflect on what we call the Nordic walk-over when it comes to gender equality. The Nordic countries, including Sweden, have long served as role models in the strive for gender equality. Gender equality has been considered an essential part of democracy. Enabling everyone's ability to take part in democracy and ensuring that all individuals have the same power to shape society and their own lives has, as we have shown, been an explicit goal for the Swedish society since the 1990s (Chapter 4). Even though the goal has not been explicitly revised since then, there are signs that the ambitious gender equality policy has been in decline. One example is that on the Swedish government's main webpage on gender equality (Gender Equality Policy in Sweden 2024) the word 'power' has been replaced by the less obliging term 'opportunities'. The full sentence reads: 'Gender equality is equality between women and men, who should have the same opportunities to shape society and their own lives.' In our view, the word 'opportunities' clearly signals a step backward in the Swedish government's ambitions.

Another, perhpas even more relevant, example is the hesitance or even reluctance to take action to counteract anti-gender hate speech and other forms of sexual violence. The offence of rape has been debated and criticised for decades, regardless of its legal definition (*Leijonhufvud* 2015). As mentioned in Chapter 6, government proposal (SOU 2023: 80) has suggested that sex or gender as a ground for hate crimes could be considered as an aggravating circumstance, but not as a protected ground under the offence agitation against a population group (*hets mot folkgrupp*). The proposal has not yet resulted in any action. A related issue, defined as gender stereotypical and therefore discriminatory against women by CEDAW and its monitoring body, is sexist advertisement. The Swedish position regarding sexist advertisement has so far been that any regulation constitutes a restriction of freedom of expression. Despite several proposals to limit such advertising through legislation the government has repeatedly concluded that it is unable to act, since such a limitation constitutes a *restriction of free speech*, as it is perceived as a protected utterance (in the form of an idea). Had it instead been recognised as a violation targeting women as a group (an act), the focus would have shifted, and the possibilities for regulation would likely have increased. The fact that the CEDAW Committee has criticised Sweden for failing to address the issue has not altered the Swedish position.

The Swedish reluctance to take action to counteract certain speech can, to some extent, be explained by the strong position of freedom of expression in the Swedish constitutional acts. Even though freedom of expression is understood as embracing both non-censorship and diversity of voices, and even though the role of the state in ensuring these aspects has resulted in a multiplicity of regulations to support both of them, when balanced against gender equality, freedom of expression is always more highly valued.

At the same time, the State has declared that more people should be encouraged to be come actively involved in democracy. The objectives of the Committee for a Strong Democracy (SOU 2022: 28) were to increase the number of people who have a good knowledge of democracy, who are involved in democratic processes, and who take a clear stance in favour of the democratic system of governance (SOU 2022: 28, 31). However, the suggested means were mainly information dissemination and opinion formation. Given the empirical knowledge we have about the silencing of women's voices, one might have expected that more far-reaching measures would have been taken.

When women's voices are silenced as a consequence of anti-gender hate speech, it has been hard for us to accept why there is such a reluctance to act. Why has the right to say whatever you want been so dominant when it comes to speech that impacts women's voices? Freedom of expression certainly has a special place in the Nordic self-image, but so does gender equality.

Having studied the regulations on international, European, and national levels, it becomes quite clear that UN, European, and EU bodies are much more radical than the Nordic countries, or at least Sweden. This insight has led us to think that Sweden has left a walk over to other actors. And, in addition, in the context of a general neoliberal, nationalistic, and conservative transformation of Sweden, this makes us even more concerned. From being at the forefront and considered a role model for gender equality, the situation is increasingly one where Sweden is losing its position and risks ending up at the EU minimum level. Sweden, and also Spain, have already received a letter of formal notice, with concerns about not properly implementing the Digital Service Act aimed at making the online space safer (see Chapter 6). The turn from role model to reluctant actor is a fact.

7.8 Conclusion

The extensive body of international and national regulation on gender equality, taken together, gives a very clear and consistent position, namely that *anti-gender hate speech counteracts gender equality* on an individual, group, and societal level. Individually, it takes the shape of physical and psychological threats and violence, causing harm and fear, also at the group level, and may, as a consequence lead to silencing of voices. The consequences are therefore societal. Silenced voices result in a democratic deficiency and run *contradictory to the democratic value* anchored in the justifications of *freedom of expression's* common good, that is, a diversity of voices. If the silencing has a gendered bias, the consequences are also contradictory to the goal of gender equality. Thus, the connection between gender equality, freedom of expression as a means to safeguard democracy, and anti-gender hate speech is clear.

At the same time, there seem to be obstacles to truly acknowledging anti-gender hate speech as counteracting democracy, and more specifically gender equality and freedom of expression. We claim that the obstacles are to a certain extent conceptual. How something is conceptualised impacts how we understand, respond to it, and how effective our measures become. We argue that it is necessary to revisit the justifications of democracy, gender equality and freedom of expression and rethink them in the contemporary societal context impacted by a different technological infrastructure than the context in which these notions were originally formulated. The digital development changes the conditions in which anti-gender hate speech takes place. We think it is necessary to rethink the very basic values of democracy to keep democracy alive. In the following, we will briefly point at the main insights from our analysis.

Anti-gender hate speech functions as both an expression and enforcer of patriarchal systems, sustained through mechanisms like himpathy and herasure. These dynamics trivialise women's experiences and prioritise male-dominated perspectives, particularly in legal frameworks that have traditionally treated gendered violence as isolated incidents rather than structural issues. While international frameworks increasingly recognise anti-gender hate speech as part of a continuum of violence against women and a threat to democracy, national implementation appears to lag behind. Sweden exemplifies both progress and persistent gaps, highlighting the tension between entrenched patriarchal norms and emerging efforts to integrate gender into hate speech regulation.

Seemingly minor acts of anti-gender hate speech, often dismissed as trivial, form part of a continuum of harm that sustains patriarchal structures and systemic inequality. These acts reinforce exclusionary ideologies and create a cultural foundation for more overt violence. Drawing on the concept of the continuum of violence, we have highlighted the cumulative impact of everyday acts, showing how they uphold structural misogyny while silencing dissenting voices. Legal frameworks, such as Sweden's gender equality policies, have begun to address these cumulative harms gaps, but gaps remain in addressing hate speech's broader cultural and ideological dimensions. Recognising anti-gender hate speech as part of this continuum is essential for promoting equality and safeguarding democratic participation.

As we have shown, the criminalisation of anti-gender hate speech must balance protecting individual freedoms with addressing structural inequalities. Resistance at the national level, often driven by strong anti-gender movements in the Western world, highlights the gap between international norms and their national implementation. What seems self-evident at the international or EU level often faces significant pushback, even in countries like Sweden, known for its radical gender equality initiatives.

As previously explained, criminalisation can be legitimised through the principle of harm, understood as both individual harm and, potentially, cumulative systemic impacts. The principle of common goods justifies limiting speech that undermines democratic participation and pluralism, while the principle of public wrongs frames hate speech as an attack on societal values such as gender equality and dignity. Yet criminal law's tendency to fragmentise – treating actions in isolation rather than as part of systemic patterns – still limits its ability to address the structural nature of anti-gender hate speech effectively.

Including gender as a category within hate crime legislation at the national level could mitigate this fragmentation, aligning legal frameworks with core democratic principles. While criminalisation alone is not a universal solution, integrating these principles can strengthen efforts to combat anti-gender hate speech and to address the patriarchal structures that sustain it.

Revisiting the theoretical justifications of freedom of expression in a contemporary context has led us to two main conclusions. First, it is essential to emphasise the importance of an understanding of freedom of expression, as not only or mainly an individual right, but also as a means for democracy and the common good. Individual rights should be exercised with responsibility. Second, measures taken to guarantee a diversity of voices should be seen as an extension of freedom of expression and not as a restriction. Freedom of expression is strengthened when a diversity of voices is safeguarded. The balance between diverse democratic values must of course be made openly and well argued. Balancing is part of most provisions of freedom of expression, even though often framed as a restriction. To perceive gender equality and freedom of expression as opposite interests is a false premise. The Swedish constitutional system for freedom of expression is an interesting example of a rich understanding of freedom of expression. We observe that this system is devalued in favour of more liberal understandings of freedom of expression, emphasising individual rights. This is precarious given the rise of anti-democratic movements. We argue that freedom of expression must be more thoroughly considered and guaranteed, as a means for democracy. And, as anti-gender hate speech threatens democratic core values, it is necessary to find ways to counteract it. We have shown that this is possible.

References

Literature

Bladini, M. & Nordisk information för kunskap om kön (2017), *Hat och hot på nätet: en kartläggning av den rättsliga regleringen i Norden från ett jämställdhetsperspektiv*. Nordisk information för kunskap om kön, Nordiska ministerrådet.

Bladini, M. (2020), 'Silenced voices. Online violence targeting women as a threat to democracy', *Nordic Journal on Law and Society*, 3(2), 1–42.
Bladini, M. & Svedberg Andersson, W. (2020), 'Swedish rape legislation from use of force to voluntariness: Critical reflections from an everyday life perspective', *Bergen Journal of Criminal Law and Criminal Justice*, 8(2), 95–125. https://doi.org/10.15845/bjclcj.v8i2.3241.
Conaghan, J. (2013), *Law and gender*, 1st ed. Oxford University Press. https://doi.org/10.1093/acprof:oso/9780199592920.001.0001.
Edström, M. (2016), 'The trolls disappear in the light: Swedish experiences of mediated sexualised hate speech in the aftermath of Behring Breivik', *International Journal for Crime, Justice and Social Democracy*, 5(2), 96–106.
Feinberg, J. (1984), *Harm to others: The moral limits of the criminal law*. Oxford University Press.
Fejős, A. & Zenta, V. (Eds.) (2021), *Anti-gender hate speech in populist right-wing social media communication*. http://genha.eu/sites/default/files/pdf/Anti-Gender%20Hate%20Speech%20in%20Populist%20Right-Wing%20Social%20Media%20Communication_0.pdf.
Franzén, A. & Gottzén, L. (2020), *Våldsprevention i Sverige: En forskningsöversikt*. Barn-och ungdomsvetenskap.
Kelly, L. (1988), *Surviving sexual violence*. John Wiley and Sons.
Kenyon, A. T., Svensson, E.-M. & Edström, M. (2017), 'Building and sustaining freedom of expression: Considering Sweden', *Nordicom Review*, 38(1), 31–45. https://doi.org/10.1515/nor-2016-0043.
Leijonhufvud, M. (2015), *Svensk sexualbrottslag: en framåtsyftande tillbakablick*. Stockholm.
Lundgren, E. (1993), *Det får da være grenser for kjønn: voldelig empiri og feministisk teori*. Universitetsforlaget.
MacKinnon, C. A. (1996), *Only words*. Harvard University Press.
MacKinnon, C. A. (2016), 'Rape redefined', *Harvard Law & Policy Review*, 10(2), 431–477.
Manne, K. (2018), *Down girl: The logic of misogyny*. Oxford University Press.
Naffine, N. (2002), 'Can women be legal persons?' In *Visible women: Essays on feminist legal theory and political philosophy*. Hart.
Richardson-Self, L. (2021), *Hate speech against women online: Concepts and countermeasures*. Rowman & Littlefield.
Speisel, C. (2024), 'Cyberhate: Medium? Message? Speech? Act? An exploration'. In Wagner, A. & Marusek, S. (Eds.), *Handbook on cyber hate: The modern cyber evil*. Springer.
Svensson, E.-M. (1997), *Genus och rätt en problematisering av föreställningen om rätten*. Iustus.
Svensson, E.-M. & Edström, M. (2014), 'Freedom of expression vs. gender equality: Conflicting values when regulating gender stereotypes in advertising', *Tidsskrift for Rettsvitenskap*, 127(5), 479–511.
Syvertsen, T., Enli, G., Mjøs, O. J. & Moe, H. (2014), *The media welfare state: Nordic media in the digital era*. The University of Michigan Press.

Court cases

European Court of Human Rights

Handyside v. United Kingdom, appl. No 5493/72, 7.12.1976.

Public documents and laws

International (UN)

Convention on the Elimination of All Forms of Discrimination against Women (CEDAW), New York, 18 Dec. 1979, entered into force 3 Sep. 1981. www.ohchr.org/sites/default/files/cedaw.pdf (accessed 2024-10-23).

International Covenant on Civil and Political Rights (ICCPR), New York, 16 Dec. 1966, entered into force 23 Mar. 1976, the provisions of article 41, entered into force 28 Mar. 1979, Human Rights Committee. www.ohchr.org/sites/default/files/ccpr.pdf (accessed 2024-10-23).

International Convention on the Elimination of All Forms of Racial Discrimination (ICERD), New York, 21 Dec. 1965, entered into force 4 Jan. 1969. www.ohchr.org/en/instruments-mechanisms/instruments/international-convention-elimination-all-forms-racial (accessed 2024-12-01).

United Nations (2019), 'UN strategy and plan of action on hate speech'. www.un.org/en/genocideprevention/documents/UN%20Strategy%20and%20Plan%20of%20Action%20on%20Hate%20Speech%2018%20June%20SYNOPSIS.pdf (accessed 2024-10-23).

International (Council of Europe and EU)

Council of Europe (2011), Convention on Preventing and Combating Violence against Women and Domestic Violence (Istanbul Convention, CETS no. 210). www.coe.int/en/web/istanbul-convention/text-of-the-convention (accessed 2024-10-23).

Council of Europe (2024), Gender Equality Strategy 2024–2029, (CM(2024)17-final), https://rm.coe.int/prems-073024-gbr-2573-gender-equality-strategy-2024-29-txt-web-a5-2756/1680afc66a (accessed 2024-10-23).

Directive (EU) 2024/1385 of the European Parliament and of the Council of 14 May 2024 on combating violence against women and domestic violence. https://eur-lex.europa.eu/legal-content/EN/TXT/?uri=OJ%3AL_202401385 (accessed 2024-10-23).

European Commission against Racism and Intolerance (ECRI) (2015), 'General Policy Recommendation no 15 on Combating Hate Speech Adopted on 8 December 2015'. https://rm.coe.int/ecri-general-policy-recommendation-no-15-on-combating-hate-speech/16808b5b01 (accessed 2024-10-23).

European Convention on Human Rights (ECHR). www.echr.coe.int/documents/convention_eng.pdf (accessed 2024-10-23).

Sweden

Gender Equality Policy in Sweden (2024). www.government.se/information-material/2019/03/gender-equality-policy-in-sweden/ (accessed 2024-08-30).

Prop. 1997/98: 55, *Kvinnofrid.* www.regeringen.se/contentassets/1733625e719c43b28f073fa9cdec90f2/kvinnofrid-prop.-19979855 (accessed 2024-11-27).
SOU 2022: 28, *Vår demokrati – värd att värna varje dag.* Betänkande av kommittén Demokratin 100 år – samling för en stark demokrati. Elanders Sverige AB. www.regeringen.se/rattsliga-dokument/statens-offentliga-utredningar/2022/06/sou-202228/ (accessed 2024-11-27).
SOU 2023: 80, *Ett starkare straffrättsligt skydd – mot sexuella kränkningar, bedrägerier i vissa fall och brott med hatmotiv avseende kön.* Betänkande av Utredningen om barns skydd mot sexuella kränkningar samt vissa frågor om brott mot kvinnor och äldre. Elanders Sverige AB. www.regeringen.se/contentassets/e8ccf3b8d03c46db856bc850e8c453dc/ett-starkare-straffrattsligt-skydd--mot-sexuella-kranknin gar-bedragerier-i-vissa-fall-och-brott-med-hatmotiv-avseende-kon.-sou-202380 (accessed 2024-11-27).

Other sources

Varieties of Democracy (V-Dem), www.v-dem.net/ (accessed 2024-10-24).

Index

FSC
www.fsc.org
MIX
Papier | Fördert
gute Waldnutzung
FSC® C083411

Kolibri 360 GmbH
Ferdinand-Jühlke-Straße 7
99095 Erfurt, Deutschland
produktsicherheit@kolibri360.de